ARTIFICE PRESENTS

THE RIBA NATIONAL AWARD WINNERS 2018

RIBA
Architecture.com

Artifice

BEN DERBYSHIRE
RIBA PRESIDENT

FOREWORD

Welcome to The RIBA National Awards Winners book, showcasing the best of British architecture in 2018. The RIBA has been celebrating outstanding work for over 180 years. Our awards and prizes are regarded internationally as a mark of excellence, recognising the best architecture, architects, research and students. Each of the winners here have gone through rigourous rounds of judging, by different jury members from award-winning practices, clients, sustainability experts and knowledgeable lay assessors.

I take this opportunity to again congratulate all of this year's winners. Their talent, hard work and ingenuity to make buildings and places that serve and enhance communities, businesses, towns and cities across the UK are a fine reflection of the superb pool of talent that exists in the profession.

May I also congratulate Artifice Press and the team behind this publication. It was clear from the outset that they placed great emphasis on crafting a book that would be consistent with the values at the heart of the awards themselves.

CONTENTS

1

HOUSES

2

CULTURE & LEISURE

3

SCHOOLS & HIGHER EDUCATION

4
HOUSING & CARE
130

5
OFFICES & WORKSPACES
180

6
SACRED & MONUMENTS
222

INTRODUCTION

JULIA BARFIELD
MARKS BARFIELD ARCHITECTS

GOOD DESIGN MATTERS. We all know that good design matters – at its best it improves the quality of people's lives, and lifts their spirits while drawing on a minimum of the Earth's limited resources. Whether it is in the design of places people call home, or where they work or learn, where they are tended to when sick, or where they play or pray, it is a powerful tool for good and has a profound impact on the kind of society we build – while also reflecting that society's values.

The RIBA National Awards are without doubt the UK's most rigorously judged and best barometer of architectural excellence. To reach the National Awards stage a staggering 230 visits have taken place involving 17 regional juries with a total of 95 jurors all giving their time for nothing – traveling approximately 3,500 miles all over the country, from St Ives to Sunderland and from Kent to Cumbria. It is a mammoth task, expertly orchestrated by the Awards team and the regional offices.

The experience for a jury of visiting a building, understanding its history and context, and appreciating the blood, sweat and tears that the architects, their clients,

their fellow consultants and the builders have put into the project, is often heart-warming and inspiring. It is also hugely challenging making those tough judgements: discerning the quality of creative thought weighed against particular challenges; involving the views of clients, communities and building users; leaving one's own architectural preferences at the door and reaching consensus with fellow jurors.

2018 has been a great year with a huge diversity and range of projects. I offer thanks to my fellow jurors and to all the architects and clients who have

THE RIBA NATIONAL AWARDS ARE WITHOUT DOUBT THE UK'S MOST RIGOROUSLY JUDGED AND BEST BAROMETER OF ARCHITECTURAL EXCELLENCE

entered the RIBA Awards this year. This book, showcasing the National Award winners, is a snapshot of architectural excellence in 2018.

Chairing the National Awards Group these past two years has been, in equal measure, a privilege, a huge responsibility and a pleasure. I am particularly pleased that the gender diversity of the National Panel has, during my time, gone from 28 per cent female to 50/50, and other jury panels are rapidly following suit.

And finally, thank you to all involved in creating this book. It is an impressive achievement.

THE JURY

The RIBA Awards Group comprises 26 of the country's top practising architects. They give their time and expertise freely to support and champion the best of British architecture. The work of this group involves desk-based assessments but crucially visiting the buildings that are in contention for National Awards and the Stirling Prize itself. Naturally, they cannot comment on the schemes their own practice has submitted, but they review, evaluate and understand several hundred projects in a typical year and cover countless miles in an attempt to find the most significant and outstanding examples of game-changing architecture in the UK.

JULIA BARFIELD
CHAIR OF THE JURY, MANAGING DIRECTOR, MARKS BARFIELD ARCHITECTS
Founding director of Marks Barfield Architects (MBA) together with husband and partner David Marks (1952–2017), they were also originators and creative entrepreneurs behind the design and realisation of the London Eye and BA i360, Brighton.

MBA has won over 80 awards for design, innovation and sustainability. Projects range from the Kew Treetop Walkway to the art-fund-winning Lightbox Woking and the University of Cambridge Primary School. Current projects include a visitor centre and HQ in the Seychelles, and the UK's first green mosque in Cambridge. As well as chairing the RIBA National Awards Panel, Julia is on the LLDC Quality Review Panel and is an external examiner at Bath University.

SIMON ALLFORD
DIRECTOR, ALLFORD HALL MONAGHAN MORRIS (AHMM)
A founding director of Allford Hall Monaghan Morris, Simon leads a studio working in London and internationally on a wide range of scales and typologies. Recent projects include the University of Amsterdam and White Collar Factory; current work includes the Post Building, Soho Place and new buildings for Google in London, Berlin and

India. Simon is Chairman of the Architecture Foundation, and has been a trustee of the Architecture Association Foundation, a RIBA Vice President for Education and Chair of Design Review at CABE. He is a frequent writer, critic, advisor and judge of competitions, and is also a visiting professor at the Bartlett and GSD Harvard.

JO BACON
PARTNER, ALLIES AND MORRISON
Jo trained at the University of Cambridge, joining the practice in 1988 and becoming a partner in 2001. She has played a key leadership role in a number of the practice's significant projects, including the refurbishment of the Royal Festival Hall, the BBC Media Village in White City, and the masterplan and two new buildings at the University of Cambridge Sidgwick Site. Currently she is project lead on 100 Bishopsgate, a 41-storey tower and associated public realm in the City. Jo is also managing partner of the practice and, in 2018, she was elected National Member to the RIBA Council.

DENISE BENNETTS
FOUNDING DIRECTOR, BENNETTS ASSOCIATES
Denise co-founded Bennetts Associates in 1987, with her partner Rab Bennetts, and plays a strategic role in the overall design direction of the practice. The practice is known for a wide-ranging portfolio of award-winning projects and has been short-listed for the Stirling Prize

twice. She is a respected architectural critic and awards assessor, serves as an external examiner at all stages of architectural education and is a member of the British School at Rome's Faculty of the Fine Arts.

TONY CHAPMAN HON FRIBA
WRITER AND CRITIC

Tony Chapman is not a trained architect but in 2011 the RIBA made him an Honorary Fellow for his contributions to architecture as a writer and film-maker, and for his work as the RIBA's Head of Awards.

Previously he made BBC documentaries about architecture. He has judged many architecture awards, including the Mies van der Rohe Prize. He is author of 20 books including two on the Stirling Prize, a children's book on architecture and three novels. He is currently doing an MA in creative writing and working on a book withPeter Zumthor and another on competitions.

NEIL DAFFIN
DIRECTOR, RITCHIE+DAFFIN

Neil is a building services and environmental engineer with a passion for architecture. He has over 20 years' experience working within the built environment at a range of scales, from development of a Zero Carbon City down to the environmental control inside a bat box. In 2013, he co-founded Ritchie+Daffin, with the aim of working on projects that marry high environmental and technical performance with beautiful architecture.

Neil has a particular interest in passive environmental design and how architecture can be developed to reduce reliance on energy-using equipment. The servicing of buildings needs to be kept simple so that much of the environmental control can be provided within the building fabric, through intelligent use of façade openings and natural light. Neil has taught environmental design to students at Cambridge, London Metropolitan, Kingston and the Bartlett Schools of Architecture.

MARY DUGGAN
FOUNDING DIRECTOR, MARY DUGGAN ARCHITECTS

During Mary's time at Duggan Morris Architects, the practice attained numerous industry awards

for design excellence including ten RIBA National and Regional Awards, three Civic Trust Awards, three nominations for the European Union Prize for Contemporary Architecture, the Mies van der Rohe Award, the Stephen Lawrence Prize, the Manser Medal and achieved consideration for the RIBA Stirling Prize for three buildings.

ANDREW GRANT
FOUNDER AND DIRECTOR OF GRANT ASSOCIATES

Andrew is a landscape architect and he formed Grant Associates in 1997 to test the creative possibilities of sustainable landscape architecture and ecological place-making. In 2012 he was awarded the title of RSA Royal Designer for Industry (RDI) in recognition of his pioneering global work in landscape architecture. He is a visiting professor for the Department of Landscape, Sheffield University, and an Honorary Fellow of the RIBA, reflecting his work on key architectural projects such as the 2008 Stirling Prize-winning Accordia. Andrew led the multi-disciplinary design team on the multi-award-winning Gardens by the Bay project at Bay South in Singapore.

ALASTAIR HALL
PARTNER, HALL MCKNIGHT

Alastair studied at Queens University Belfast and Cambridge University. He worked for Grafton Architects before returning to Belfast where, in 2003, he co-founded the practice that is now Hall McKnight. The practice has offices in Belfast and London – with projects in the UK, Europe and further afield. Their work has been recognised through both national and international awards.

ABIGAIL HOPKINS
DIRECTOR, SANEI HOPKINS ARCHITECTS

Abigail Hopkins is a founding director of the practice Sanei Hopkins Architects. Abigail studied architecture at Columbia University, New York. After a spell working in New York, she returned in 1992 to London to join Hopkins Architects where she worked on a number of diverse projects including Jewish Care in North London, Saga Headquarters in Folkestone and the Forum Building in Norwich. In 2000, she went on to co-found Sanei Hopkins

Architects with her architect husband, Amir Sanei. Since then she has attempted to balance having five children with a busy practice life.

MARCUS LEE
PARTNER, LEEP

Marcus Lee is the founding partner of Leep Architects. He previously founded FLACQ after 21 years at the Richard Rogers Partnership. He was site architect on Lloyd's of London, then led Heathrow Terminal 5 and Madrid Barajas airport competitions. He had a key role leading a number of high profile regeneration projects – Greenwich Peninsula and the Millennium Dome (O2) and other mixed-use residential schemes such as Bjorvika Oslo, Brentford Waterside, Bethnal Green Gasworks and Embassy Gardens Nine Elms. The redevelopment of the Nestlé factory in Hayes, student hotels in Italy and award-winning experimental houses are part of a diverse range of projects in recent years. Marcus has collaborated with a number of architects leading ECOM's successful bid for A pier Schiphol. He is a Design Council/CABE panel member.

ALEX LIFSCHUTZ
DIRECTOR, LIFSCHUTZ DAVIDSON SANDILANDS

Following a degree in sociology and psychology and research in cognitive psychology, Alex studied at the Architectural Association in London – and many years later he served as its President.

In 1986 he formed Lifschutz Davidson Sandilands, and the firm has gone on to win awards for its varied commissions – community and arts buildings; office, residential and mixed-use schemes; public realm and innovative structures; plus the regeneration of the South Bank and new suburbs in emerging areas of London.

Alex recently edited *Loose-Fit Architecture, Designing Buildings for Change*, picking up on his interest in architectures that develop over time.

STEPHANIE MACDONALD
DIRECTOR, 6A ARCHITECTS

Stephanie Macdonald founded award-winning architecture practice 6a architects with Tom Emerson in 2001. The practice is best known for its critically acclaimed contemporary art galleries, educational buildings and artists' studios. Recent work includes the new South London Gallery Fire Station, Cowan Court, Churchill College, Cambridge and Coastal House. In 2017 the Juergen Teller studio was shortlisted for the RIBA Stirling Award and 6a architects' El Croquis architectural monograph was published. In 2012 she jointly received, the Schelling Medal for Architecture. In 2018 Stephanie was nominated for the Women in Architecture Awards.

JO MCCAFFERTY
DIRECTOR, LEVITT BERNSTEIN

Jo leads the practice's major housing studio, overseeing residential projects of all types and scales from inception to completion. With vast experience of designing and delivering housing, her key role has been to champion inventive design solutions at masterplanning and detailed design scales – an approach that has been rewarded with many competition-winning schemes and industry accolades, including RIBA Awards.

In parallel with architectural projects, Jo advises on design and quality standards through her involvement in various design review panels and as a CABE Built Environment Enabler. She also participates in mentoring programmes and is a guest critic and invited lecturer at various universities.

STUART MCKNIGHT
PARTNER, MUMA

MUMA (McInnes, Usher, McKnight Architects) was established in 2000 and since then has delivered a number of high-profile public arts projects. The principals of MUMA met when they studied together at the Mackintosh School of Architecture in Glasgow. Stuart's professional experience is almost entirely in complex public and cultural projects, often in historic settings, and he has spoken on these themes at lectures and conferences around the world. He has been a specialist advisor to juries for RIBA design competitions for museums and galleries.

TRACY MELLER
PARTNER, ROGERS STIRK HARBOUR + PARTNERS

As lead architect on projects such as LSE Centre Buildings redevelopment, NEO Bankside and Mossbourne Academy, Tracy has a track record of delivering innovative schemes on some of the most complex urban sites. Having joined the practice in 1999, she was made a partner in 2016 and has been involved in a wide range of projects at all stages, across the residential, commercial, healthcare and education sectors. In addition to her role in the RIBA Awards Group Tracy has been a judge for the AJ Awards, AJ Women in Architecture, WAF and the Civic Voice Awards.

KATE MURPHY
PARTNER, FOSTER + PARTNERS

Kate Murphy, architect, is a partner of Foster + Partners with over 20 years of experience on a variety of project types and scales ranging from cultural buildings to high-rise towers and workplace design. Her particular speciality is the regeneration of historic buildings to give them a sustainable future. High-profile projects include joint project lead for Bloomberg London and the redevelopment of the Museum of Fine Arts, Boston, as well as key roles on competition submissions for Oceanwide Center in San Francisco and Imperial War Museum London.

JOHN PARDEY
DIRECTOR, JOHN PARDEY ARCHITECTS

John Pardey established his practice in 1988 and has gone on to win 47 national and international awards.

He has held lecturing posts at the South Bank, PCL, Canterbury and Portsmouth Schools of Architecture. He was a member of CABE's National Design Review Panel from 2009. He has been a member of the National RIBA Awards Panel since 2015. John is the author of three books: *Utzon: Two houses on Majorca*, 2005, *Louisiana and Beyond – The Work of Vilhelm Wohlert*, 2007, and *Peter Aldington: Houses*, 2016. His new book *20 Great Houses of the 20th Century* is to be published in Spring 2019.

GREG PENOYRE
PARTNER, PENOYRE & PRASAD

Greg Penoyre is co-founder of multiple award-winning London architectural practice, Penoyre & Prasad, which has gained a reputation for distinctive architecture with a strong commitment to sustainable design. He brings to the practice a lifelong interest in the art and craft of design and has played a central role in the design, procurement and delivery of the practice's 300-plus projects.

Greg regularly serves on design review panels, and as an architectural assessor of competitions. He is an active member of the RIBA Awards Group and judge of national and international awards, and is currently a visiting professor at the University of Sheffield.

ANNALIE RICHES
DIRECTOR, MIKHAIL RICHES

Annalie Riches is a founding director of Mikhail Riches, a practice specialising in residential and mixed-use projects across a variety of scales and tenures. The practice has won several RIBA Awards for its built work, and RIBA London Building of the Year in 2013.

MARIA SMITH
FOUNDING DIRECTOR, INTERROBANG ARCHITECTURE AND ENGINEERING

Maria Smith is a London-based architect working across architecture, engineering, journalism, education, awards, and events. She is a director of architecture and engineering practice Interrobang, and Webb Yates Engineers. Prior to this, Maria was a director of multi-award-winning art and architecture practice, Studio Weave. She writes a monthly column for the RIBAJ, is a member of the RIBA National Awards Panel, a trustee of the Architecture Foundation, and one of the Mayor of London's Design Advocates. Maria also co-founded the international series of politics and architecture debates, Turncoats, and is chief curator for the Oslo Architecture Triennale 2019.

AMIN TAHA
CHAIRMAN, GROUPWORK

Amin was born in Berlin and lived for a short period in Baghdad before settling in London. While in the offices of Zaha Hadid, Wilkinson Eyre and Lifschutz Davidson Sandilands he gained experience and friendships, entering and winning a small number of competitions that allowed them to begin independent practice. GROUPWORK is an employee ownership trust whose principals include Elisa Lam, Dominic Kacinskas, Dale Elliott, Jason Coe and Alex Cotterill. A handful of projects have been completed, each a recipient of a RIBA Award with one shortlisted for the Stirling Prize.

JOANNA VAN HEYNINGEN OBE
FOUNDER OF VAN HEYNINGEN AND HAWARD ARCHITECTS, NOW CONSULTANT

Joanna van Heyningen founded her practice in 1977 and formed van Heyningen and Haward Architects with Birkin Haward in1982. She was involved on all van Heyningen and Haward's award-winning buildings, including those for higher education, particularly in Oxford and Cambridge, further education and schools. She has worked with the National Trust, the RSPB, English Heritage and Transport for London.

Joanna has always sought to contribute to the wider built environment, and has been involved with RIBA in several capacities, including being a judge of the Stirling Prize, and now on the Awards Group. Over many years she has been a design review panellist at CABE, for which she co-chairs the Oxford Design Review Panel. She is governor chair of the Building Committee of the Purcell School of Music.

She was awarded an OBE for services to Architecture and the Built Environment in 2016.

PAUL VELLUET
PRINCIPAL, PAUL VELLUET, CHARTERED ARCHITECT – CONSERVATION, DEVELOPMENT AND PLANNING

Paul Velluet is a chartered architect with some 40 years working in both private practice and the public sector – including ten years as regional architect for English Heritage, London – specialising in building conservation and development in historic areas. In 2005 he established an independent consultancy specialising in the provision of professional and technical advice to property owners, prospective developers and other planning and building professionals on projects involving

new development in historic areas and the conservation, alteration and extension of historic buildings. Currently, he serves on the Archdiocese of Westminster Historic Churches Committee and the Guildford Cathedral Fabric Advisory Committee, and he served on the Cathedrals Fabric Commission for England between 2005 and 2010.

JANE WERNICK CBE
CONSULTANT ENGINEERSHRW

Jane is an engineer who likes to work on projects that give delight. At Arup since 1976, she ran their Los Angeles office from 1986–1988. Her most notable project was the Millennium Wheel (London Eye). In 1998 she founded Jane Wernick Associates (JWA). Projects include the Young Vic, the treetop walkway at Kew Gardens and the Living Architecture Houses. In 2015 JWA was incorporated into engineersHRW. Jane has taught at many architecture schools. She won the 2013 CBI First Woman of the Built Environment Award. She is a member of various design review panels, and think tanks, and edited the RIBA Building Futures book, *Building Happiness – Architecture to Make You Smile*, 2008.

CHANTAL WILKINSON
PRINCIPAL, WILKINSON KING ARCHITECTS

Chantal studied at the Royal College of Art. She is a principal of Wilkinson King Architects, which she runs with Julian King. In addition to the RIBA Awards Group, Chantal is a member of the National Trust's Historic Environments Advisory Group and a design advisor for Hackney Borough Coucil. She has taught architecture over many years at several universities including Cambridge, Kingston and Syracuse London.

1

HOUSES

HOUSES

House building has become a testing ground for some of the country's most experimental architecture: a chance for design-literate owners to take risks

One thing that sets apart private house architecture from most other areas of architecture is that it's often a chance to throw off the shackles of convention and try something new. The client isn't a business or a corporate concern, interested in maximising floor space or following design regulations. As private individuals they are prepared to take risks and are often very design-literate: interested in aesthetics, keen to try new ideas. As a result houses are, for architects, an opportunity for experimentation and invention. There is a kind of freedom that you don't get in any other kind of building.

Indeed, a couple of houses on RIBA's regional shortlist – Vex, an oval-shaped concrete house in Stoke Newington by Stephen Chance and Wendy de Silva, and Makers House in Hackney by Liddicoat and Goldhill – were actually designed by the architects for themselves. You can see how they both used the opportunity to experiment with materials and design details.

The private houses in this category are very varied, in terms of materials and approach. There are houses in brick, stone, concrete and timber. As a result it's hard to pin down a unifying trend. In part this is because of the extreme variety of size and location, as well as whether or not the project deals with existing built fabric. There seems to be a particular interest in using natural materials to give architectural articulation, colour and texture, and a delight in pattern making.

One thing that unites the best private houses is that they all successfully respond to their surroundings using natural site-specific materials and designs that work with the local environment. In an urban setting you're looking

at the conversation the building is having with other built form around it, and how its design and massing mediates with the street and fabric of the city. With rural houses there is a conversation between the house and the landscape, immediate and distant.

For instance, the Old Shed New House by Tonkin Liu in Yorkshire is based around an old farm shed. They've retained the existing metal structure, albeit with a few changes, to purposely keep the contextually sympathetic barn aesthetic. It's surrounded by birch trees, so the cladding of the new shed is designed to echo the verticality of the trunks and also the patina of the bark itself. It also includes a quite remarkable library, a double-height space, which unites

I AM HEARTENED BY HOW ALIVE AND HEALTHY THE STATE OF PRIVATE HOUSE BUILDING IS IN THE UK, JUDGING BY THESE AWARDS

the ground and first floors and is overlooked from the bedroom areas. Because the owner wanted to leave some shelf space for the future, but was concerned that the library would appear empty, they put mirrors behind all the shelves. It's a wonderful experience – the library space seems to shimmer with sparking light, endlessly reflected around the room – it's quite disorientating!

The Lochside House, on the south shore of a sea loch on the west coast of Scotland, is set in a breathtaking, ancient rocky landscape close to the water's edge. Nestling into the trees, its plinth is made of stone while the cladding is timber. Entirely comfortable in its immediate context, its elemental form echoes the distant mountains, seeming to pull

them closer to form a striking composition in nature. Large windows, towards the loch, give dramatic views looking out to the mountains, while carefully placed windows, both high and low, on the other side, create picture-frame views into the trees.

Flexibility is quite important, although design briefs are often archetypal. The open-plan space is still very popular, and it's something you'll find in the Flexible House in West London. It has the shell of a 1950s terraced London house, where the interior was cleared of all existing structural elements, including downstand beams, to be re-inhabited with a series of floor-to-ceiling spaces lined in cherry wood. Several of these are moveable and can be used to partition

the rooms in different ways. The detail and craftsmanship is extremely high quality. The floors are unified by the wonderful carved stone stair, rising from the basement, with its delicate tensile balustrade that spirals up through the house.

The Coastal House in South Devon is another very beautiful property where the clients had lived on the site for a long time. The existing house was, in fact, two linked together, and it took a while to understand how to open up the existing spaces to find rooms that would give the clients the house they wanted. Lowering the ground floor level gave them a good datum to work from. It's an extremely intelligent reworking, exposing the existing fabric to form

wonderful living spaces, and opening up views across the plan and to the beautiful Devon landscape. All of the interventions are very carefully considered. The existing large stone walls are left exposed internally, but pointed and painted. There are elements of new intervention, such as a wonderful timber column in the living room, whose shape is echoed in the spindles of the stairs.

I am heartened by how alive and healthy the state of private house building is in the UK, judging by these awards. I'm impressed by how many clients want to build or improve their own homes, and by how much effort they are they are prepared for in order to achieve their dream. Partly I think it's the number of TV shows on the subject!

COASTAL HOUSE

6a architects

CLIENT: PRIVATE
LOCATION: DEVON
PHOTOGRAPHY: JOHAN DEHLIN

The transformation of this early twentieth-century house, located close to the South Devon section of the South West Coast Path, is breathtaking in its elegant restraint

AFTER OPTIONS WERE explored for complete reconstruction of the building, it was decided to retain much of the original structure. Wrapped in an external insulating 'duvet' and faced in reclaimed slate, the result is a house which feels rooted in place, and which is both rich in history and also full of contemporary detail and delight. The exterior gives few clues to the extent of the reinvention – an elegant oak-framed veranda and the curious ovoids which punctuate the deep lead fascia are the only immediate indications of what lies within.

The interior has been reinvented by the removal of one of the four original chimney stacks. New openings are framed in board-marked in-situ concrete, and a winding timber stair rises through the central three-storey, top-lit atrium, creating a series of balconies and terraces to an extraordinary interior landscape. Walls are generally painted, coursed rubble. A silken maple handrail on raking oak balusters winds around the central space. At ground level the floor level has been dropped to connect inside and out, elongating existing windows and creating a grand scale for the more public rooms. A cross-axis at the centre of the plan aligns with views out in every direction, framing the stunning coastal prospects and shorter aspects into an inner courtyard. Externally Dan Pearson has created a series of landscapes which mediate from rolling clifftop to walled gardens – his terrace on which the new veranda rests comprises shallow, honed slate steps and riven risers.

This project has emerged from several years of dialogue between client and architect, and a brave change in direction well into the design process. The scheme both respects and reinvents the original house to create a timeless and beautifully made new home.

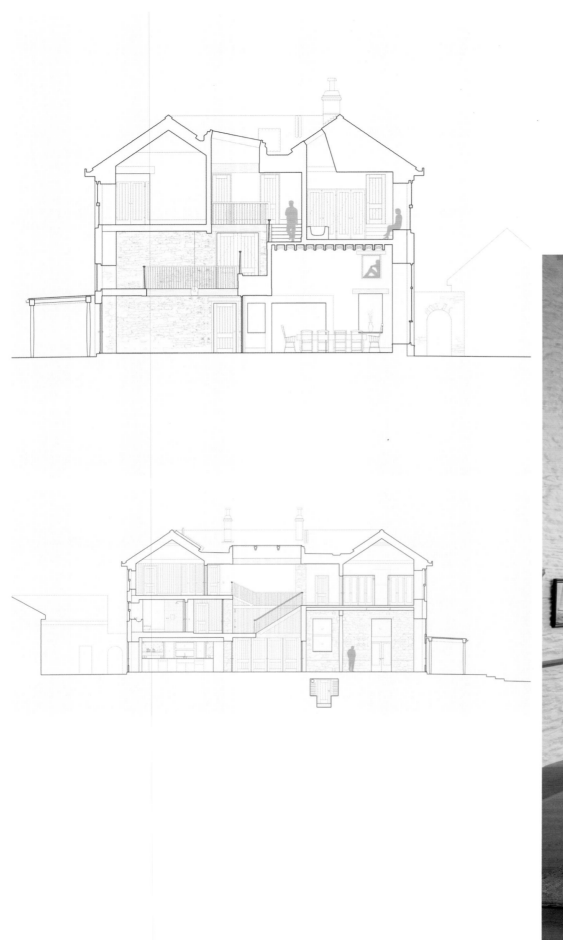

OLD SHED NEW HOUSE

Tonkin Liu

CLIENT: PRIVATE

LOCATION: YORKSHIRE

PHOTOGRAPHY: GREG STORRAR, ALEX PEACOCK

Discovering the site with their son Greg, now Associate at Tonkin Liu, and Mike Tonkin, the architects sought to pull the landscape into the building's form

THE CLIENTS HAD spent several years looking for a quiet site to build their retirement home, before they found a farm shed located in a wild garden, on the edge of a small village in North Yorkshire.

A long double-height gallery maintains the tree-lined approach, and a tall library, bounded by mirror-backed shelving, evokes the copse of silver birches found on the site. Walking into the library through a sliding door from the living room draws gasps from the first-time visitor. It is the heart of the home and a centrepiece for a lifetime's collection of books. Clever use of light and mirrors give the impression of an art piece itself. Otherwise it is a modest three-bedroom

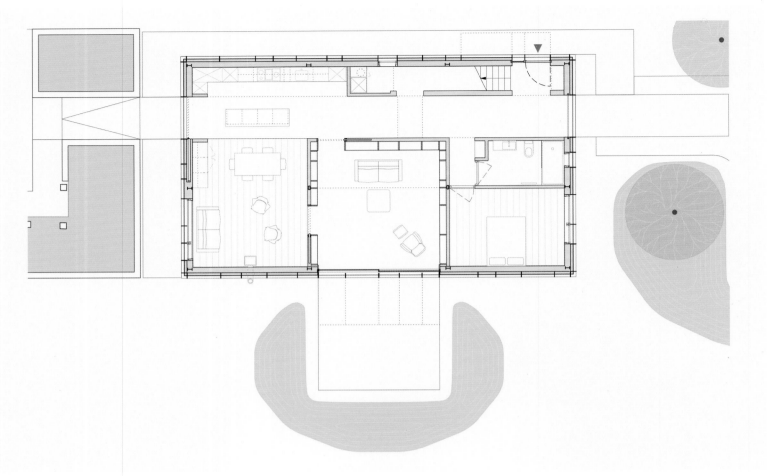

house, built cost-effectively, but with exquisite detailing throughout, inside and out.

The house follows a Passivhaus strategy of high insulation and high air-tightness, complemented by mechanical ventilation with heat recovery. Timber louvres are neatly integrated into the design of the timber cladding to limit solar gain in the south-facing library. Larch cladding of various widths has been shot-blasted and stained white between galvanised steel fins to offer a rhythmic façade that reads like the bark of the silver birch trees. Galvanised steel also features inside, with a delicate mezzanine and bridge, using only 80 mm structural-depth, and delicate timber joinery in every room.

The colour scheme of subtle grey tones, concrete screed floor and white shaded timber seems to effortlessly complement the art collection in every room. As the architects say, "The house is a journey of interconnected spaces that alternate between the grand and the intimate… it is part country cottage, part classical villa."

FLEXIBLE HOUSE

Amin Taha + Groupwork

CLIENT: PRIVATE
LOCATION: LONDON, NW1
PHOTOGRAPHY: TIM SOAR

Even before entering this refurbishment of a suburban home, one can see a tribute to the finest architectural craft

THE METALWORK CUT meticulously into its front door will remind any architect of Carlo Scarpa and Mies van der Rohe – and the architect of this West London jewel is more than happy to proclaim and accept that association.

Designed around the clients' use of the building and its possibilities in plan and section, that the resulting three-dimensional space is moulded from a love of material is evident, wherever one pushes, pulls, looks or moves. If serious architecture can be fun, this is the house that confirms it.

In such a small and unassuming shell the architect has created a flexible home on all levels. With hinged cabinetry and walk-through bathrooms, this carved-out cave is a delightful living experience.

Everywhere you tread, this building is more than the sum of its parts. The extension to the rear offers a place to sit, work or dine, while allowing light into the basement. The structure of this bench and extension is thermally broken through a bespoke metalwork crosshair of angles that also supports an elegant arm which conceals the tethered but moving light fittings underneath.

Residential balustrades will never be viewed again in the same way. An elegant cobweb of wire threads through the gravitas of a structurally independent and beautiful stone stairway, and defines the aperture, to allow in light at roof level and dissipate it as the stair alights at lower ground level. Furthermore, if you need a fire escape from here, why not make it a wine cellar so you can grab a drink on the way out?

In its playfulness of use but also in its love of material and detail this is significantly ambitious architecture. Stone is used in multiple textures, both underfoot and overhead, and concrete is textured to match, bringing a continuous yet rich feel from top to bottom of this 300m² home. It's like living in a medieval stone workshop.

This home is designed around the clients' needs, the architects' love of material and their ability to manipulate space, and it has delivered what can only be described as a tour de force. The intelligent humour and confidence of this building is infectious... and it makes you smile.

LOCHSIDE HOUSE

HaysomWardMiller

CLIENT: PRIVATE
LOCATION: SCOTLAND
PHOTOGRAPHY: RICHARD FRASER

The setting for this house and garage/studio building is where its name suggests: the south shore of a west coast sea loch, on a peninsula of grass and heather moorland, in impressively hilly surroundings

SHELTERED FROM STRONG winds by pine trees and larches, the house faces south across a small bay.

The house itself consists of three volumes, the individual scales of which are inspired by the historical remains of buildings on the peninsula which date back to Mesolithic times. These interior spaces are connected by a circulation area beneath a green roof planted with sedums, sea plantain and sea pinks from the rocks nearby. The faithful reliance on the immediate surroundings for inspiration extends to local materials (such as the dry-stone walling, which uses stone quarried from mere miles away), and the intention has been to create a house that can fit naturally into this ancient landscape.

Due to the house's remote setting, energy efficiency has been a vital consideration. Good insulation, triple glazing, roof-integrated solar thermal and PV panels, battery array, thermal store and ventilation heat recovery all help the building to run autonomously for some of the year, further helped by a wood-fired stove/boiler and generator during colder periods. Interior spaces are lofty and light, divided by a lower circulation spine, and make the house feel warm and comfortable in all weathers.

This highly successful creation by the team of architect, client and builder impressed the judges. The scale, material choices, use of the setting and integration into the landscape were all excellent. A sustainable building making good use of wood was a delight to visit. The care in the design and in the building of this house makes it an exemplar of its genre.

2
CULTURE & LEISURE

CULTURE & LEISURE

In the area of culture and leisure, be it a gallery, museum, theatre or sporting arena, the best buildings need to be defining spaces with a sense of cultural permanence

What a building needs to succeed differs with each project. To have achieved a National Award a level of excellence will have been agreed by the assessors against a number of criteria. One thing that should be highly valued is whether a project has been able to retain its ambitions throughout its design and construction. Projects can begin with the best of intentions, but it takes a high degree of commitment from the clients, investors, architects and end users for that to be maintained. Many projects will begin with worthy and important ambitions but somehow along the way those values can become eroded or compromised and so such projects may not achieve their full potential.

In the area of Culture & Leisure, we can look at recent projects like the [2016] Stirling Prize winner Newport Street Gallery, or 2012's [shortlisted]

Hepworth Wakefield gallery. There's such a high degree of endeavour and commitment that has driven projects like these – making places with a strong cultural identity. Such projects value the idea of permanence. That doesn't necessarily mean a physical permanence but having a cultural permanence, a sense of becoming a defining cultural space or institution. How do we know if a building can do this? That is a fair question. Awards tend to be bestowed early in the life of the building, perhaps before we can be sure of its ability to endure beyond its immediate impact. Perhaps a process might develop where a longer-term view around the lives of buildings is considered through the Awards programme. As architects, we can consider the projects presented to us and take a view as to their ability to physically

endure the effects of time, but it's trickier to assess how a project's cultural life will proceed.

One thing that has been very interesting in this group of buildings is the prevalence of projects which are effectively extending or working with existing structures and spaces. There are only two projects that you might identify as standalone new-builds – the Storyhouse in Chester and the Nucleus in Scotland. The others, to varying degrees, are all working with an existing set of architectural circumstances, whether it's the V&A Exhibition Road Quarter, Liverpool's Royal Court, the New Tate St Ives or the two projects at the Royal Academy of Music. This could speak to a wider economic sensibility in terms of clients expressing a responsibility for existing buildings and places over which they already have

stewardship rather than necessarily creating something completely new. Tate St Ives is an interesting example in this respect, as it extends an existing building in such a way that it now feels complete – somehow, and very positively, both the new addition and the original project seem to support each other in such a way that it is difficult to consider them separately. The existing galleries house a permanent collection where the architecture and the collection of objects have become embedded in each other – but the new exhibition gallery offers the curators an ability to accommodate widely different modes of occupation.

We previously talked about the idea of permanence, and most of the projects in this chapter (that is to say the ones which have been extended or added to in some way) have already endured for some time

and are now entering a new period in their history. I think that is something that is perhaps different to recent decades. Architectural culture has become more comfortable to work with a certain modesty, and many of these projects have an understated, dignified quality to them.

For new or emerging architectural practices, the RIBA Awards are particularly important. For one thing, it can reassure clients and validate their commitment to have commissioned a project that achieves an award. As architects we can be very good at congratulating each other and being aware of who is doing what, but clients need to be rewarded and recognised as well. In respect of that, it's important to note that a RIBA Award is not for an architect, it's for a project – and a committed client can be just as vital to the process.

PEOPLE ARE GENUINELY INTERESTED IN THE LIVES OF BUILDINGS AND THE CULTURAL VALUE THAT A PROJECT CAN BRING TO A PLACE RATHER THAN JUST ITS INITIAL VISUAL AMBITION

I think there can be a degree of presumption that architects are always seeking to be radical, to do something visually arresting, but that is just one view. There is an established sensibility in contemporary architectural culture that values the longer lifespan of a building over any immediate visual impact. This chapter speaks of that to some degree. A number of these projects are visually powerful, but some are more understated and invite a slower, more considered engagement over their life. People are genuinely interested in the lives of buildings and the cultural value that a project can bring to a place rather than just its initial visual ambition. There's a humility and also a sense of public service to some of these projects, and perhaps that sense of service to a place and to the users and public is part of what will give such projects an ability to endure.

NEW TATE ST IVES

Jamie Fobert Architects with Evans & Shalev

CLIENT: TATE ST IVES

LOCATION: ST IVES, CORNWALL

PHOTOGRAPHY: HUFTON + CROW, GRAHAM GAUNT

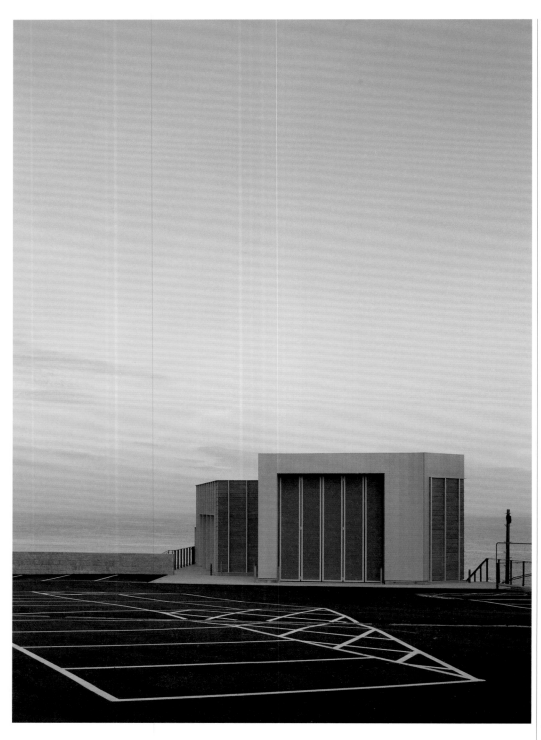

The visible manifestation of the new building is minimal and modest, underplaying its impact on the interior experience for visitors and staff

THE EXTENDED GESTATION of the reconfiguration and extension of Tate St Ives has resulted in a building with more than twice as much gallery space, which resolves the functional challenges of the original building, increases the car parking provision at the top of the site and creates an enhanced public route from top to bottom of the site.

Externally the most prominent feature is the faience-clad loading bay – visible from Porthmeor Beach, the subtle greenish-grey ceramic turret sits unassumingly between Evans & Shalev's original building and its adjacent housing. The gallery extension has been carved out of the hillside, connecting seamlessly to the existing galleries; the top-lit space is capped by deep, in-situ beams which create a rhythm and character very different to the 1990s spaces. From the loading bay, soaring etched-glass doors give access to a huge goods lift which connects all floors, and also provide enhanced disabled access to the gallery. In addition, provision of a new picture store and workshop enhances functionality. A winding in-situ staff stair with lacquered steel handrail celebrates simplicity while also connecting a new, upper level staff entrance to offices, a meeting room and a staff amenities space, which enjoy stunning seaward views. The granite and glass gallery roof lights lead into a public landscape of granite paving and planting which pays homage to the nearby cliff tops.

The evolution of this iconic south-west attraction has encountered huge challenges, overcoming vociferous local stakeholders and significant site constraints. In terms of architectural ingenuity, a building has been delivered where there appeared to be no site available, with minimal intrusion on an already crowded horizon. It has created an intriguing new public landscape, giving pedestrians a connection from hilltop to beach – and, with subtle reordering of the original gallery, it achieves a seamless environment in which to enjoy art.

THE PIECE HALL AND CALDERDALE CENTRAL LIBRARY AND ARCHIVES

LDN Architects

CLIENT: CALDERDALE METROPOLITAN BOROUGH COUNCIL
LOCATION: HALIFAX
PHOTOGRAPHY: LDN ARCHITECTS, PAUL WHITE

The new library is a bold addition, beaming with civic pride and connecting to the Piece Hall

THE PIECE HALL is a Grade I listed unique and iconic cloth hall, dating from 1779. It was built for the trading of 'pieces' of cloth (30-yard lengths of woven woollen fabric produced on a handloom) and would have been open for business every Saturday between the hours of 10.00 am and 12.00 noon, so trading for just two hours each week.

This level of commercial activity was presumably not very sustainable, and the building has had a number of uses throughout its history. It had been in decline for a number of years, and in the early 2000s its future was in doubt. Since then, Calderdale Metropolitan Borough Council has promoted the Piece Hall as a cultural, creative and community focus for the region. LDN Architects won the project through public procurement, and project architect Mark Hopton has been making almost weekly visits from Edinburgh for 15 years.

As a conservation project every stone of the building has been carefully reviewed and repaired or replaced with appropriate restoration skills. But it is in the transformation of this building where the design team and client's ambition has stood out. Previously the spaces were unheated, and the

scheme includes new infrastructure and building services to deliver high-quality commercial space for new businesses operating in shops and cafés. A new entrance (a so-called fourth gateway) has been added into the historic courtyard, which for the first time has created permeability from the town centre to the railway station. Visitor numbers have soared.

Part of the site is occupied by the Square Church, some of which was destroyed by fire and demolished in the 1970s. The church's surviving tower and spire dominates the Piece Hall courtyard. The new Central Library and Archive occupies the space of the former church, and blends the remains of the stone fabric within its layout. It is a modern facility with automated book sorting, media store, flexible community spaces and a world-class document archive built to the higher environmental standards. The original rose window has been delicately restored with double-glazed units cut to fit. Externally the new library is a bold addition, beaming with civic pride and connecting to the Piece Hall.

ROYAL COURT, LIVERPOOL

Allford Hall Monaghan Morris

CLIENT: ROYAL COURT THEATRE TRUST
LOCATION: LIVERPOOL
PHOTOGRAPHY: TIM SOAR, ROB PARRISH

The Royal Court is a popular theatre but receives very little funding and had been in a run-down condition. Here we see a difficult urban site become more civic and welcoming

DURING A PROJECT lasting over a decade, the theatre and its urban setting have been transformed into a welcoming, sustainable venue. The architect has brought a sustained and intelligent commitment to the project, with a carefully phased programme of 'three acts' allowing the theatre to remain open throughout construction, all except for three months. Operational flexibility and a real sense of welcome, delight and even theatrical grandeur have been achieved on a very modest budget, through skill, ingenuity and some hard editing.

The new foyer is a simple, bold and logical replacement of the original cantilever canopy, with the AV billboard allowing the building to be stripped of advertising clutter. A difficult urban site has been made more civic and welcoming. The foyers benefit from a well-judged strategy combining stripping back and the retention of the best historical fabric. The raw distressed aesthetic works as a fine foil to the more luxurious original material and – together with some bold interventions – combines to create an atmosphere appropriate to the occasion: open, welcoming and sufficiently grand but without pretension or extravagance.

This commercial theatre has been able to expand its social programme with a basement studio theatre and bar carved from a set of subterranean rooms. The backstage area has been given dignified and decent facilities. This is astute conservation, in keeping with the spirit of the building and its function as a hard-working venue, in which a contemporary form of theatrical grandeur is achieved on a low budget.

STORYHOUSE

Bennetts Associates with Ellis Williams

CLIENT: CHESHIRE WEST AND CHESTER COUNCIL
LOCATION: CHESTER
PHOTOGRAPHY: JOHN MALTBY, PETER COOK, MARK CARLINE

THE SYNERGY AND efficiency of the overlap of public spaces, through night and day, has been well exploited. The building offers a diverse range of connected spaces, ranging from the intimate to the grand and theatrical, and achieves a continuous activation and accessibility to a very broad constituency of users.

The spaces are comfortable and clearly well liked and used, benefitting from the attention paid to acoustics and ceiling heights, and the creation of pockets of space within a big suite of connected foyer spaces. The overall strategy is clear and robust – the theatre is new and intersects with the retained and revealed shell of the previous cinema – with a very theatrical use of the original proscenium.

A children's library occupies the high street facing former shop front – creating a charming suite of rooms – at once visible and highly inviting from the street, yet intimate and comfortable, usable by large or small groups.

The project is a convincing response to the question of how to activate a town centre through day and night, and of how to make culture fully and widely accessible. While taking cues from successful commercial spaces (bookshops and big pubs), the project succeeds in creating a new atmosphere for a cultural venue – refreshingly free of commercial trappings, and delivering cultural access to people very much 'on their terms'.

In a piece of radical robust conservation, the project is an interesting and relevant new combination of public building typologies – theatre and library

The theatre design is a radical solution to the flexibility required by the organisation and its business model, namely to show both home-grown productions and larger touring shows. The theatre can morph from an 800-seat proscenium to a 500-seat thrust stage in an ingenious low-tech way. This involves erecting a new stage within the main space – and undertaken twice a year this is cost-effective. The layout and structure have been cleverly resolved to give excellent sightlines and a comfortable well-proportioned hall in either configuration.

The highly theatrical stairs and bridges that access the theatre also serve a studio theatre and bar at the top of the building, in a nice move that creates a celebratory rooftop destination with a different ambience. Excellent back-of-house facilities include long views across the distant landscape.

Externally the treatment is bold and well judged. The new brickwork is a sensitive complement to the original, an inventive interpretation and not a slavish copy. A robust cast-glass screen befits the scale of the building, opening to axial views predicating the wider connectivity in the emerging masterplan.

WALTHAMSTOW WETLANDS

Witherford Watson Mann Architects / Kinnear Landscape Architects

CLIENT: LONDON BOROUGH OF WALTHAM FOREST
LOCATION: LONDON, N17
PHOTOGRAPHY: JASON ORTON, HEINI SCHNEEBELI

The Walthamstow Wetlands have been created out of an area of 200 hectares that previously had only limited accessibility and that locals considered a wasteland.
It now very successfully links four London boroughs and has opened up a beautiful expanse of land and waterscapes for public recreation

THE COLLABORATION BETWEEN client and architects involving multiple stakeholders and specialist consultants has been exemplary, fulfilling an opportunity to develop, fundraise and deliver a vision that exceeded the brief. The intention was to provide amenities needed to allow public access to the site, with new paths, bridges and cycleways now crossing the area with clearly signed entrances and new facilities, including two original buildings.

The sensitive handling of the restoration of these historic buildings using a simple palette of materials has been particularly successful. The careful detailing and sourcing, from bricks to wooden panelling (even old school chemistry desks reclaimed as tables), contrasts well with the new steel gantries, stairs and lifts to access the viewing platforms. The main visitor centre is situated in the old disused Engine House, which has the extra attraction of a new brick swift and bat tower – an addition to the original brief and a real benefit to the scheme. The disused Victorian Coppermill Tower has been converted into a second viewing platform further along the route.

Graphically the signage and wayfinding is well thought-out, using a variety of materials and methods to underline the industrial past of the site: three-dimensional metal signage at the entrance; lettering studded into the paths; and the word 'wetlands' picked out in brick on the swift tower, making it a local landmark.

The site has already attracted many more visitors than the original forecasts predicted, hopefully giving rise to the possibility of additional enhancements in the future. The scheme, which encompassed four separate contracts, highlights an intelligent integration of architecture and landscape to create a new public space.

ROYAL ACADEMY OF MUSIC – THE SUSIE SAINSBURY THEATRE AND THE ANGELA BURGESS RECITAL HALL

Ian Ritchie Architects

CLIENT: ROYAL ACADEMY OF MUSIC
LOCATION: LONDON, NW1
PHOTOGRAPHY: ADAM SCOTT

This extraordinary project fulfils the client's pipe dream for ideal accommodation, within the confines of occupied Grade I and II listed buildings

IT REPLACES A 1970s auditorium in the very heart of the Royal Academy of Music, while also adding a new auditorium with a completely different ambience, at rooftop level, This project has been technically complex: structurally, acoustically and logistically. Its resolution has a contemporary feel, that sits very comfortably within its historic setting, much of which is freshly revealed. As a result the Academy has acquired world-class performance spaces for the enjoyment of its students and of the public.

The Susie Sainsbury Theatre is a new performance space for Britain's oldest conservatoire. The new theatre, designed for both opera and musical theatre, provides over 300 seats, through the addition of a balcony. This is 40 per cent greater capacity than in the auditorium's previous incarnation and, along with the addition of a large orchestra pit, stage wing and full fly tower, miraculously transforms the level of performance and teaching the Academy can provide.

The theatre has a warm, sensual quality, its faces lined in meticulously detailed faceted cherry wood, into which Liverpool red seats are embedded. The architect has explored how wood is transformed and tuned, as well as the role of varnish and pigments in Stradivarius's instruments. The timber lining has been manipulated to provide good sound reflection and diffusion, as well as warmth and light. The client is delighted that the acoustic effect meets the design aspirations, and the expert first audience confirmed that it enhances and refines the sound qualities as beautifully as intended. The auditorium lighting, a metaphor for an exploded chandelier and a

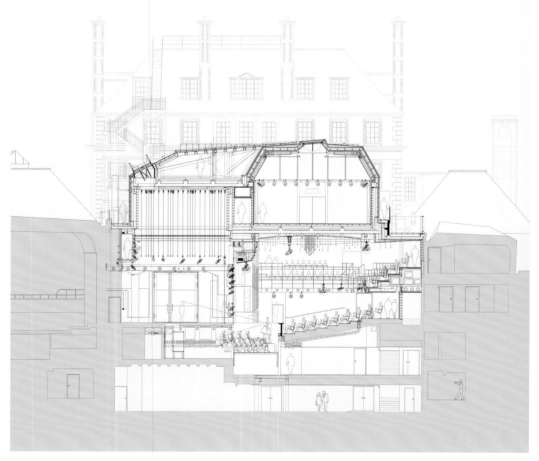

galaxy, complements, and is integral to, the dramatic theatricality of the space.

The new 100-seater Angela Burgess Recital Hall, sited at rooftop level, exploits the last major area into which the Academy could expand. The setting, among the rooftops of listed buildings, was very sensitive. Clad in Nordic blue pre-patinated copper specially developed for the project, the recital hall visually merges with the new fly tower to create a unified form that fits well into its surroundings and is imperceptible at street level.

Lined in pale, exquisitely detailed limewashed oak, the recital hall is tranquil, calming and visually cool. An oculus provides a central focus and its expressed construction is intended as a reference to the tension and tuning mechanism of stringed instruments.

Full disabled access has been provided throughout the building, and the alterations enhance the historic building, with naturally lit stairs and the previously concealed Grade II listed rear façade revealed. Formerly bricked-up windows have been replaced, allowing natural light to permeate through parts of the building that had been rendered windowless. The building is very well sealed and insulated, and has a highly efficient building management system, with combined heat recovery and air-source heat pumps.

In all, this is a very accomplished piece of architecture, which resolves exceptionally complex technical challenges, with elegance, wit and aplomb.

SHAFTESBURY THEATRE

Bennetts Associates

CLIENT: THE THEATRE OF COMEDY COMPANY
LOCATION: LONDON, WC2H
PHOTOGRAPHY: ADAM SCOTT

This powerfully dramatic addition to the skyline of London's West End is a feat of architecture, engineering and prowess

TO REMAIN COMPETITIVE in theatreland the Grade II listed Edwardian theatre needed a retrofit to extend its performing capabilities. This was achieved by adding a new fly tower, to increase flying capacity from 12 to 35 tons, with new offices and plant rooms. The work entailed erecting a new structure, interlaced within the existing building to carry the exceptional new load at the top of the building. Piles were driven 28 metres down, incidentally near to Crossrail lines and an underground river. Columns were threaded through the existing structure, and steels craned and spliced into place, while the 1,400-seat theatre remained fully operational, and with residential neighbours next door, sharing party walls.

The result of these efforts is a terrific new facility for theatrical performance. Historic features have been retained, such as the capacity to open the auditorium roof. This used to be relatively common in the West End but is now only possible in the Shaftesbury Theatre.

The new fly tower at roof level is encircled by rudimentary staff offices, which have a strong ambience of back-of-house. They have been arranged to form a stepped profile, to avoid direct

sunlight and overheating, and to break down the bulk of the new extension, when viewed from outside (both at street level and above). The effect when viewed from afar is a sculpted, stepped, corten steel structure which, when lit at night, hovers like solid illuminated banners over the roof of the theatre. Day and night, the form and colour resonate strongly with the red brick and faience of the original building and its neighbours. Though clearly contemporary, it sits very comfortably in its setting.

The effect of the works has been to reduce the theatre's operational costs. The existing boiler plant in the basement has been replaced with a new roof-mounted packaged boiler plant room with high-efficiency condensing boilers. These serve the whole theatre and have reduced energy and NOx emissions. Air-source heat pumps provide all the heating and cooling required, with offices naturally ventilated.

The briefing and design development were carried out by the design team working directly with the client. The success of this complicated project is a reflection of the excellent relationship between the client and architect, who are continuing their creative working relationship by co-developing the next phase of improvements at the Shaftesbury Theatre.

VICTORIA AND ALBERT MUSEUM EXHIBITION ROAD QUARTER

AL_A

CLIENT: THE VICTORIA AND ALBERT MUSEUM

LOCATION: LONDON, SW7

PHOTOGRAPHY: HUFTON + CROW

Every once in a while an architect, a site and a client work seamlessly together to create a special moment in the city. The new courtyard, café, shop and gallery of the Exhibition Road Quarter is such a place in time

APPROACHED VIA EXHIBITION ROAD itself, significant alteration to a Grade I listed screen has opened up the new V&A entrance to the Albertopolis vision of a close relationship with the Science and Natural History Museums. Crafted aluminium gates, drilled with reference to previous damage to the screen, and the royal association to the institution behind, open up to a new threshold space in the city which delights with movement, light and culture.

This extremely sensitive and constrained site is manipulated, carved and folded to overcome significant difficulties with regards to topography, entry and the scale of new gallery space to be provided and serviced.

Surfaces roll, kink and step to create a comfortable and welcoming entrance sequence. Enveloped by the beauty of the existing buildings and screen, the exquisitely detailed ceramic tiling reflects brightly in the sun and captures crisp shadows in southern and western sunlight of the ornate cornicing and columns that surround the space. This free-flowing architecture is at peace with the intricacies of the plan and sectional challenges of this site, and its fluid form sits in comfortable contrast to the verticality and formality of the buildings that hold its edges.

The decision to remove rooms internally – to allow views through to the inner courtyard – places the new entrance in an enviable position, between a classical courtyard and a contemporary one. From here a staircase cut into the floor dives and curves into the bowels of the construction, past an enjoyably expressive community of columns supporting the heavy masonry above.

On arriving at the lower ground floor, one finds the soffit of the new gallery itself is suggestive of the playful court above, and in its creases allows in

natural light as required. The structural expression is folded into the movement of the stair and court above, creating a continuous journey through an aesthetic that makes a whole of the multiple issues arising from building under, within and very close to the existing listed buildings. The whole composition flows effortlessly.

Servicing is from a narrow gap in the city block to the north, and the sub-basement is carefully arranged around security and process requirements; a joy to the managers and curators of the space.

Exit is via the shop, as one would expect, but this space is more than just retail – it opens up connections to adjacent galleries and affords views into the beautiful circulation of the existing V&A buildings. A glazed panel is cut at an acute angle delicately into the stonework of the existing buildings – an example of the incredible attention to detail upon which this kind of intervention depends.

Materials are kept to a minimum but are handled with aplomb: ceramics to the court and café roof and timber flooring, and a carefully chosen grey to the galleries. The deep black dynamic stair in varying gloss and matt finishes for ergonomic and cleaning purposes is a real delight.

The difficulties both in spatial and conservation terms for this project may well have seemed unassailable, but the choice of architect and associated project have proven to be a wonderful decision. The project is a clear example of how a contemporary architectural piece can not only enhance the city through material, space and contrast, but can also be a fluid, expressively elegant response to problem-solving in the most difficult of situations.

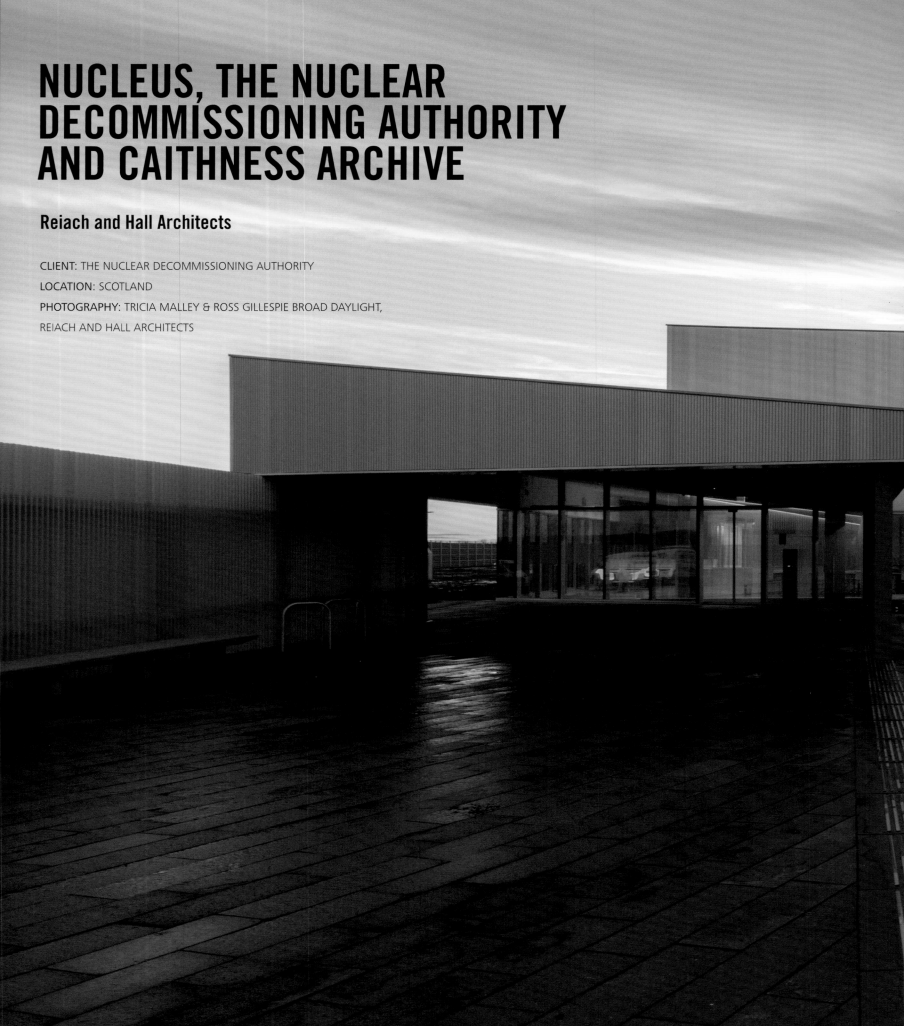

NUCLEUS, THE NUCLEAR DECOMMISSIONING AUTHORITY AND CAITHNESS ARCHIVE

Reiach and Hall Architects

CLIENT: THE NUCLEAR DECOMMISSIONING AUTHORITY
LOCATION: SCOTLAND
PHOTOGRAPHY: TRICIA MALLEY & ROSS GILLESPIE BROAD DAYLIGHT,
REIACH AND HALL ARCHITECTS

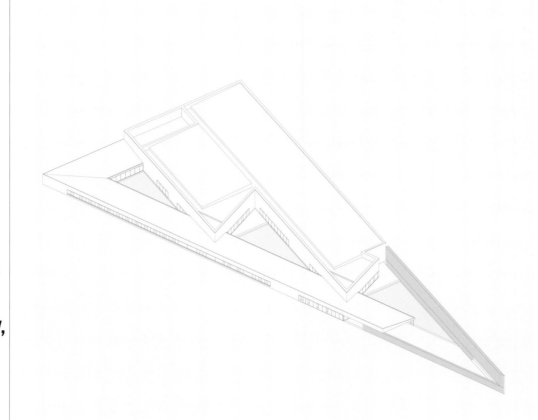

Situated near Wick's airport, Nucleus resembles an industrial shed coupled with administrative offices in a wild, exposed location, but its aim has been to attract and welcome the local community, the expert and the visitor

THE NUCLEUS BUILDING acts as a holding space for two archives. One is the national archive for the Nuclear Decommissioning Authority, which details the physical and digital documentation of the UK's civil nuclear industry from the 1940s onwards. Its bold triangular shape, which relates in part to the locale's geography, was inspired by Caithness writer Neil M Gunn, whose work addressed the relationship between community and the universe. The public and archivist spaces are divided from the larger archive holding spaces by triangular water courts. These courtyards also bring light and ventilation into the building area.

The building of archive material – which preserves it and allows access to it – consists of a vast double-height cellular concrete construction layered with a double-skin roof, which is both protective and environmentally stable. The single-storey public and administrative building occupies a light-filled open-plan enfilade wing of lightweight construction, and its cladding – made from extruded silver anodised aluminium and vertical louvres – responds well to the changes of light common in this region of far northern mainland Scotland. Overall, the lochans highlight the building area as forming part of the relationship between landscape and light.

This was an impressive industrial building and also an ethereal and beautifully sculpted one, especially given the security of the landscape. The relationship of the building to the historic context of the site and the adjacent wartime airfield, together with the references to the Caithness context of lochs and a difficult climate, are beautifully articulated.

3

SCHOOLS & HIGHER EDUCATION

SCHOOLS & HIGHER EDUCATION

Schools and colleges need to be considerately designed spaces that consider light quality, acoustics and connectivity in order to remain welcoming and exciting to every new cohort of pupils

Altogether the National Award is about excellence in architecture, and all of these educational buildings are excellent and inspiring. Educational buildings particularly need to endure as exemplary pieces of architecture despite, in many cases, having to triumph over very low budgets. Educational buildings are among the most important projects that any architect can undertake, and there's a growing understanding about what a good educational building should look and sound like.

They are community buildings and they need to be legible and to withstand a lot of wear and tear. For each cohort of pupils or students who arrive for a new academic year, these buildings need to remain welcoming, exciting and delightful. It's essential that they don't look shoddy after a few years. There is an annual turnover of users and you don't want them to be disappointed by what they find. They have to excite each generation, and those generations move on pretty quickly.

They can't just be rugged, they have to lift the soul. They must feel fresh and daylit on a gloomy November Thursday afternoon. That's why they must have really wonderful qualities of light, which is what so many buildings in this chapter have got. The other important thing is acoustics. They need a calm acoustic environment, and when I look at these buildings I can see acoustic treatments all over the place in all of them. The Royal Birmingham Conservatoire obviously

needs to think about acoustics as it's a concert hall, but you also have something like Boroughmuir High School in Scotland, which is a very big school with a huge number of pupils, but is also a delightful place to be partly because it has terribly-well controlled acoustics, so it can handle masses of people.

I think for places to be inspiring there must be a sense of space going beyond a single room, a sense of connection. Kingsgate Primary School has, very intelligent use of space, so internal spaces lead to external spaces, which in turn lead to the community at large. How these buildings relate to the city or town is important to their success. Storey's

THERE'S A GROWING UNDERSTANDING ABOUT WHAT A GOOD EDUCATIONAL BUILDING SHOULD LOOK AND SOUND LIKE

Field Centre and Eddington Nursery is magical. It's a real community building par excellence, not just in the sense that it welcomes the community, but in that it stands there in west Cambridge as a civic building, playing a role well beyond its brief. It has real ambition for what a building can be.

There is definitely a difference between schools and higher education spaces, so somewhere like the Sultan Nazrin Shah Centre at Worcester College, Oxford, is a building for adults. It's a very expensive and outstandingly beautiful place of contemplation and coming together for serious grown-ups. West Court at Jesus College, Cambridge is

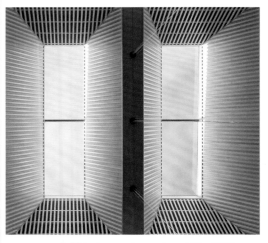

similarly a place for grown-ups to meet and discuss. It's also a very good use of an existing building.

But you are always trying to do the same thing, which is inspire and delight. What you are doing is trying to make a good space for human beings, with rooms for them to congregate, to be quiet in, for meetings. Education has specialist needs but it's essentially for people to gather. Educational trends also change, and buildings have to be able to deal with that. That means making spaces that aren't too specific, but which can be made specific by the user. It's also about the structure – having a framed structure rather than load-bearing walls

– that means you can really mess around with the internal walls when you need to.

Schools don't need to intimidate, but they do need to ensure they don't over-excite. In planning and material there should be a sense of orderly calm. That's really important. The kids can provide the disorder but the buildings should bring a feeling of order. As a group, they all have a sort of gravitas about them, even the primary schools. Whether they are for primary education or secondary, or further education or music or sport, they have a quiet authority about them. They are all thoughtful, intelligently planned and really delightful buildings.

STOREY'S FIELD CENTRE AND EDDINGTON NURSERY

MUMA LLP

CLIENT: UNIVERSITY OF CAMBRIDGE
LOCATION: CAMBRIDGE
PHOTOGRAPHY: ALAN WILLIAMS

THE SPACES IN the nursery are worthy of a much more sophisticated audience, but are always based around the scale and activities in each space. Where small windows are needed they are arranged in the pattern of constellations of stars (even with the correct orientation), and where a decorative circular window from the enclosed garden is made out of a ventilation inlet grille, it is evidence of the skill, imagination and constant attention to detail of the architect. This is a truly well-crafted building – material or technology is only used where it is needed.

The community centre and nursery are linked operationally, so that a sense of space from views of the playground, daylight and ventilation are brought into the café but without compromising the privacy of the children. Where spaces have dual uses, like the external garden outside the wedding venue, which can be used as a quiet reading room for the nursery, the competing needs of the users are balanced and the management of the building is happy to make the extra effort (opening doors or moving furniture) to make it all work.

The community hall itself has been designed to become a more important place in the new community at Storey's Field, to become its civic centre or town hall. It offers opportunities for weddings, music concerts, funerals or political

This is architecture of the very highest quality. It shows how an architect can add joy, an enhanced experience of materials and human dimension to every part of a building

debate, which puts it ahead of a space for hobbies, exercise, local groups and kids' parties. To address this enhanced symbolic value for the community, the architects stepped the building sideways to address a longer view in the masterplan, and set it back to create a gathering space outside the hall and a parents' drop-off space outside the nursery. To complete the sense of civic pride, the external walls of the hall are lined with comfortable seats to stop and chat to neighbours while you wait to enter.

The inside of the hall is a beautiful balance of function, sustainability (it is vented naturally using an underground labyrinth), acoustic performance and expression of materials. The patterned brickwork of the enclosing wall acts to break up the reflections of music or speech to provide good acoustics, but also suggests patterns of geology in the surrounding landscape. The amount of daylight or the feel of the acoustics can be changed by simply dropping or raising blinds, so users can control the environment without complex management systems. Even the access stair to the plant on the roof is via a sculptural spiral staircase that takes its part in performances.

This is an example of the very best in British architectural design – when it is this good it offers ideas, skill and care in ways that transform the human use and experience of this building at every opportunity.

KINGSGATE PRIMARY LOWER SCHOOL

Maccreanor Lavington Architects

CLIENT: LONDON BOROUGH OF CAMDEN
LOCATION: LONDON, NW6
PHOTOGRAPHY: TIM CROCKER

Part of a mixed-use masterplan for this former industrial estate in West Hampstead, Kingsgate Primary School demonstrates a strong collaboration between architect and client to create a surprisingly generous inner-city school

THE SCHOOL, TOGETHER with a new public space, is significantly set back from the street, providing an intelligent urban design solution for parents to drop off and pick up without causing congestion on the residential street. The public space also opens up a new connection to the neighbouring park, which was once a dead-end and underutilised green space.

The large covered entrance to the school offers glimpses into the playground while providing a protected environment for the children. The distinct roofline of the saw-toothed and double-pitched roofs pays homage to the industrial past. This is also

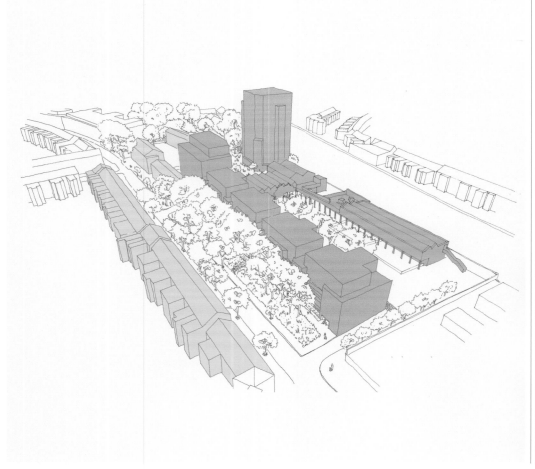

picked up in the children's drawings of the school. It also helps to bring excellent levels of daylight through the north clerestory windows into the teaching spaces, offering a spacious and serene quality throughout the school.

The arrangement of classes and circulation encourages the children to move through open spaces, and connection to the outdoors is framed at every turn with generous windows.

The robust, lightly stained timber surfaces and panelled walls conceal storage spaces, and a careful layout of lobby areas for cloaks and storage also buffer the space between the ground floor classrooms and the outdoor play space during colder periods.

In amalgamating circulation with breakout spaces, the architect has strived to make them work hard and in many different ways without compromising calmness.

The grand assembly hall is impressive and reminiscent of the scale of a Victorian school hall with its huge volume and pitched roof. However, this is much warmer and far better acoustically! It is flexible and can be divided and used as a dining and sports hall with plenty of integrated storage space for equipment to be tidied away.

Kingsgate makes successful use of the site, within a carefully considered masterplan that addressed the adjacent railway line and benefits from a southern aspect, creating a 'connected' public space.

Owing to this careful layout of the site, the flexibility of key spaces in the school with the use of the wider community has a real chance of success. Above all, a laudable procurement of the school design is tailored to the client's vision and the pupils' needs, and one senses that the children attending this school are off to an exceptional start in education.

MARLBOROUGH PRIMARY SCHOOL

Dixon Jones

CLIENT: THE ROYAL BOROUGH OF KENSINGTON AND CHELSEA

LOCATION: LONDON, SW3

PHOTOGRAPHY: PAUL RIDDLE

The community created in school buildings is paramount to the educational outcome of the children that attend

MARLBOROUGH PRIMARY SCHOOL, formed through a convoluted planning negotiation, transforms an urban site into a series of terraces that wonderfully defines a school culture centred around daylit space and external play space.

A complex diagram in plan and section, the school teaching spaces surround places of congregation, linked to a central stair arrangement and joining bridge. Orientation and connections are carefully orchestrated around the activities of the building to ensure that the daily lives of both teachers and students are enhanced.

Entry and security are handled with care, with students enjoying a vertical external journey to their classrooms in the morning and visitors welcomed at the opposite corner with close access to the main vertical circulation core.

A series of levels and variable screens offer the ability to make communal spaces for different scales of event, and steps and an internal ramp offer a place to rest and a dynamic experience throughout the centre of the plan.

Circulation routes are kept short and active, with shared learning spaces creating a happy hierarchy of places for learning with views to the outside. Long views prevent an institutionalised feel and create variety in a school day.

Year groups are cleverly separated by level; pupils quite literally rise through the school with varying treatments to their external spaces which face south-east, culminating in a multi-use games area on the roof that is enjoyed by other users out-of-hours, which leads to welcome wider community engagement.

Externally the school creates important permeability through the site with its adjacency to a commercial building by the same architect. The heavy context of brick buildings is mimicked by this piece of architecture, although with a deftness of touch the elevations are treated with a fresh colour and geometric openings that subtly suggest the different use inside.

The impressive sectional diagram and solid detailing of this school creates an impressive new urban block, linking the school to the city while providing a terraced place of learning that is readable, fresh and distinctive. It is a school that will encourage pupils to play, learn and achieve.

BOROUGHMUIR HIGH SCHOOL

Allan Murray Architects

CLIENT: CHILDREN & FAMILIES DEPARTMENT, CITY OF EDINBURGH COUNCIL
LOCATION: EDINBURGH
PHOTOGRAPHY: DIMITRIS PANAGIODITIS, ALLAN MURRAY ARCHITECTS, KEITH HUNTER

Situated on a steeply sloping urban brownfield site next to a canal, the relocation of Boroughmuir High School in Edinburgh has been a waterfront project dictated by limited space, and it has used these constraints in various ingenious ways

ARCHITECTS AND CLIENT have co-operated in rethinking how a school maximises space, for teaching, social and community, and how the use of light and natural ventilation can make interior spaces feel less cramped and more comfortable for its staff and pupils. From small classrooms to larger sports halls, not a single square metre of space could be wasted, and that has led to a great deal of innovation.

Concrete construction with exposed soffits enabled more thermal energy to be embedded. The creation of a rooftop multi-games area (MUGA) and confining all PE accommodation to one building has made transportation of pupils around the school area more practical. Externally, similar limited space between the school building and the nearby canal has resulted in a natural plaza acting as an entrance to the school, which feels both expansive and safe. A community park space and outdoor gym also exists in this area.

This was an exceptional project – very impressive compact planning, allowing for large well-lit spaces. Excellent acoustic treatment and a very intelligent strategy concerning safety around fire, smoke and ventilation has meant that neither of the large multi-height atria are enclosed by walls or screens. The plan and section are rational, legible and ordered. There is an excellent relationship between inside and out at both main levels, and the public realm has been beautifully handled.

THE SULTAN NAZRIN SHAH CENTRE

Niall McLaughlin Architects

CLIENT: WORCESTER COLLEGE
LOCATION: OXFORD
PHOTOGRAPHY: KEITH BARNES, NICK KANE

The setting for this building is unbeatable. It is situated beside a perfectly mown cricket pitch within the secluded, rambling and idyllic garden of one of Oxford's most historic colleges.

TO NOT ONLY preserve but enhance this context would require a building of assured calm and grace. It would need to use materials with a tactile gravitas and be imbued with a timelessness to make it feel as if it had always been there and need never leave. The Sultan Nazrin Shah Centre does all this and more.

It was not an easy path to get here. Worcester College had an urgent need for the teaching facilities it contains, but had to prove that there was nowhere else in its capacious campus to accommodate them, and demonstrate that they could be built without harming the floodplain, the adjacent trees or the matchless setting. It has taken time, requiring unstinting application from the client and the procurement team, a generous donor prepared to cover the eye-watering build cost, a building team capable of the highest levels of craftsmanship, and an architectural team capable of the very highest design quality.

The result is a building of extraordinary elegance. In bald terms it is a relatively small single-storey teaching facility, with an auditorium, seminar rooms, a dance studio and ancillary facilities, all arranged around a generous central foyer which opens onto a stepped terrace addressing the cricket pitch. But above and beyond this, every space is high-ceilinged and flooded with daylight, every element is designed

and crafted to the most exacting tolerances and standards, and every part fits together sweetly – from the radial brick pavers to the curved seats and huge oak doors of the auditorium up to the spaces themselves, formally arranged as discrete stone forms around which the forum flows.

The building is classical in spirit, with crisp proscenia and a slender stone stoa marching along the cricket pitch façade. However, it is uncompromisingly modern in style, with smooth planes of stone and glass and minimal detailing. Yet there is nothing alien or mechanistic about it; in fact its craft is surprisingly traditional, relying on stonemasons, plasterers and joiners at the very top of their game. It is the natural materials, superbly honed, that ground the building and make it belong. It is the architectural design – the timeless pursuit of ordering space and light and form – that makes it a thing of pure joy.

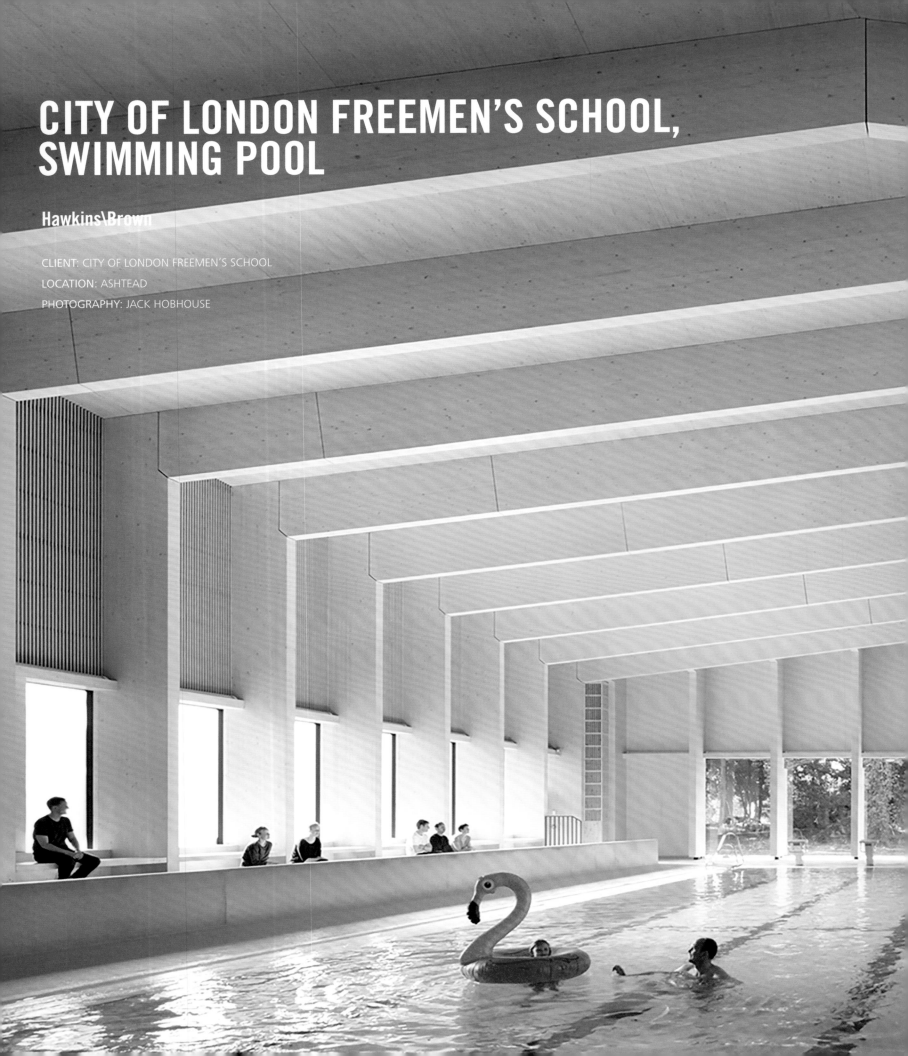

CITY OF LONDON FREEMEN'S SCHOOL, SWIMMING POOL

Hawkins\Brown

CLIENT: CITY OF LONDON FREEMEN'S SCHOOL
LOCATION: ASHTEAD
PHOTOGRAPHY: JACK HOBHOUSE

The new swimming pool replaces the previous one, which was located elsewhere on the campus and which recently burned down

THE MASTERPLAN, BY the same architect, had to be revisited and so offered the opportunity to better locate the new pool away from the Grade II listed house and closer to other sports facilities.

The pool building has a sensitive location: it is set within the green belt, the curtilage of Grade II listed buildings and adjacent to ancient woodland. The architects have responded by creating a quiet, unassuming building from the outside, which is practically invisible as you approach from the house. They utilise the sloping site to their advantage, creating a simple, low-lying form, clad in a dark brown zinc panelling. Few hints are given to what one experiences upon entering the building.

By contrast, the pool interior is light and spacious with a cathedral-like quality. We experienced it when not in use, so it exuded a supreme tranquillity and calmness, which was heightened by the beautiful views out across a meadow to the woodland beyond. The pool is at the same level as the ground outside: on two sides, windows drop down to the floor to create the sensation of swimming with nature.

The predominant internal material is timber, with white-washed glulam frames and CLT panels – all well detailed and finely crafted. The proportions and spatial arrangement of the main pool interior are elegant and pleasing. Quality is high throughout – the M&E is virtually invisible within the main pool space, which is no mean feat.

The success of this project is a testament to the trust and good relationship between the client and architect, particularly evident in the way they worked together to overcome challenges.

SIBSON BUILDING

Penoyre & Prasad

CLIENT: UNIVERSITY OF KENT
LOCATION: CANTERBURY
PHOTOGRAPHY: QUINTIN LAKE, TIM CROCKER, IAN GOODFELLOW/PENOYRE & PRASAD

The new campus building is the largest on the site and houses the School of Mathematics and the School of Business

THIS IS A very thoughtful building, with a clear architectural concept which has been rigorous enough to withstand the project development and budgetary constraints. The concept of zigzagging wings helps to integrate the two schools while allowing them to have their own dedicated spaces. The central atrium is embedded in the middle of the zigzag and serves not only to bring the two schools together to use the shared facilities such as the café and lecture theatres, but also to welcome the wider campus.

The wing concept extends the building across the site, increasing its surface area to maximise the views and to break down the mass of the building. Set within an area of ancient woodland, the wings dissipate into the surrounding trees, offering a delightful and uplifting experience from inside the building. The verticality of the anodised aluminium fins on the external cladding further heightens the blurring of trees with the building.

Natural light pours into the top-lit atrium, which provides a welcoming entrance and place to socialise. When the jury visited it was busy and vibrant, with circulation carefully choreographed around pausing spaces. Inside the atrium, the concrete structure is exposed and finished to a very high quality and, together with the timber glulam beams, brings a lightness and elegance not usually seen in an education building of this scale.

These materials are expressed similarly in other public-facing spaces, such as the lecture theatres and, to a lesser extent, the shared breakout spaces which break the length of the corridors.

The quality of detailing is impressive, particularly as the contract was design and build. It was evident that the relationship between the design team and the contractor was good, with shared aspirations helped by good communication of design intent. Likewise, there seemed to be a strong sense of trust and respect between client and architect, and when we met them the architect's passion and enthusiasm was infectious. We found it enjoyable to hear them speak about their ideas and we felt this was an impressive team collaboration.

Overall, this is an exemplary educational building, embodying creativity with an intelligent and responsible approach.

THE DAVID ATTENBOROUGH BUILDING

Nicholas Hare Architects

CLIENT: UNIVERSITY OF CAMBRIDGE

LOCATION: CAMBRIDGE

PHOTOGRAPHY: ALAN WILLIAMS, TOBY SMITH, NICHOLAS HARE ARCHITECTS

This building represents a true working partnership between the original architects, Arup Associates led by Sir Philip Dowson, and successors Nicholas Hare Architects

WHAT HAS HELPED give the building a new lease of life is the change in use of the upper floors from closed laboratories and offices to the light-filled, open-plan offices for the Cambridge Conservation Initiative, a worldwide assembly of international research and green lobby groups led and supported by Sir David Attenborough.

The architects have treated the building fabric with the utmost respect; repairing and cleaning concrete, matching window detailing, and replacing the lead cladding with a matching aluminium panel while recognising the shortcomings of the public access areas and the windswept first-floor circulation spaces. This clear thinking has focused change and architectural intervention on the ground and first floors, where new grand stairs are combined with a ramp to reach the first-floor entrance. The whale skeleton which has hung outside for nearly 50 years was taken down, cleaned and is the centrepiece for the new entrance pavilion, shop and meeting space for school trips that creates a new front door at ground level.

The structural frame and external form of the building has been carefully retained where it looms over the rooftops of Cambridge city centre, but opportunities have been taken to create a new vertical circulation space, resplendent with an entirely appropriate 'green wall'. This intervention enables shared meeting rooms and breakout spaces

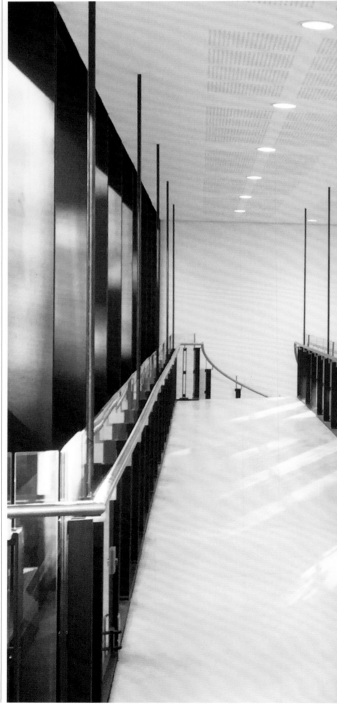

for each of the organisations that come together in the Cambridge Conservation Initiative, while allowing them their own front door and 'brand' identity inside their open-plan offices.

The architects explained how the new tenants did not share their enthusiasm for exposed concrete, so the office spaces have had to be handled in a more neutral way. On the lower floors the original building is returned faithfully to its original finishes and the Museum of Zoology (still a work in progress) has restored the original Dowson Interior.

The transformation of what used to be called the Arup Building is the first step in opening up this crowded part of the university to Cambridge city centre so that the café, shop and museum will all become busy destinations for the public. In the meantime, this is a first-rate example of how the integrity of a modernist building can be retained, and its future protected, by a clear-headed conversion to new, highly appropriate uses.

The repair and restoration of modern classic buildings require so much more skill, care and research than more common conservation projects. At the David Attenborough Building the architects have used all the traditional conservation skills but have also connected with the spirit and muscularity of the original building.

WEST COURT JESUS COLLEGE

Niall McLaughlin Architects

CLIENT: JESUS COLLEGE
LOCATION: CAMBRIDGE
PHOTOGRAPHY: PETER COOK, NICK KANE

This extension to Jesus College manages the difficult trick of feeling entirely old-fashioned in its use of hand-crafted materials like oak, elm, red clay floor tiles and a soft red brick, while remaining entirely modern in its loose geometry, use of daylight and simplicity of forms

THE BUILDING FACING onto Jesus Lane extends an existing structural frame (the Rank Building) by two floors, providing hotel rooms to generate income for the college. By setting back the top part of the elevation where it faces the traditional Cambridge court it completes the parapet line of the existing buildings. Meanwhile on the street side, the complete four storeys rising from the back of the pavement are appropriate to the scale of the street.

This level of judgement, sensitivity and design skill is carried through each separate intervention in the college complex; where the north elevation delicately steps between the two different scales, it is completed by huge oak timber-framed windows.

The transition to the adjoining building is achieved with the 'pivot' of a tower or a 'lantern' – a motif repeated from the Summerhill College (Oxford) scheme but enhanced and enlarged. The stair dramatically wraps around the lantern, resolving complex circulation from the street to the courtyard and the playing fields beyond. Again, there is imagination and invention in the detail where the stair flares out in plan as it reaches the ground floor, to welcome the visitors.

A walk through the building reveals further alterations, extensions, excavations and updates. A new lecture theatre/conference centre is sunk into the basement but still lined in elm, and is side-lit by windows to the street; the faithful replacement of a damaged gable end, reuses the reclaimed stone framing to the window; and a lightweight café/bar provides a more relaxed social space, with a noisy bar and performance space tucked underneath.

Even the introduction of a microbrewery is entirely in the spirit and tradition of a Cambridge college. Everywhere the architecture is based on the use of weighty materials with a surface, colour and texture of their own. Jesus College now offers a sequence of rational, thoughtful spaces that seems inevitable, but we know took a great deal of architectural skill and determination to deliver.

ROYAL BIRMINGHAM CONSERVATOIRE

Feilden Clegg Bradley Studios

CLIENT: BIRMINGHAM CITY UNIVERSITY
LOCATION: BIRMINGHAM
PHOTOGRAPHY: HUFTON + CROW

The first purpose-built music college built in the UK since 1987, the new Conservatoire represented not only a rare opportunity to create a state-of-the-art facility fit for the digital era, but also to anchor Birmingham City University's expanding city centre campus with a building of civic stature

SPECIALIST INSTITUTIONS OF this type sometimes discourage public access but here, with the client's positive endorsement, the architects strove to make the building feel as accessible as possible. This is evident immediately upon entering the three-level foyer, which connects entrances on the north and south sides of the building. If externally the building's brickwork carapace lends it the air, in the words of the architect, of an 'urban castle', defending the delicate music-making from traffic

gives way to an alternating rhythm of timber verticals and black geometric ripples, again determined by acoustic considerations, producing an aesthetically pleasing pattern that gives the hall a serene gravitas.

Upper floors, the more private realm of students and staff, accommodate practice rooms, sound laboratories, classrooms and recording studios; a finer grain of spaces that had to be carefully reconciled with the large volume of the concert hall extending upwards from below. The architectural choreography of the Conservatoire's complex brief, and its range of different spaces, has been handled with a deft touch – clear testimony to the close collaboration of architect and client team, producing a building that not only enhances the school's educational reputation, but is surely destined to become one of Birmingham's most actively used and cherished public venues.

noise, the split-level foyer with its timber lining is a warm, welcoming space for students, staff and the public to mingle. A café, looking out onto campus gardens, reinforces the informal, convivial atmosphere. With its generous processional stair, reminiscent in a less formal way of a grand opera house staircase, the foyer links together the Conservatoire's signature performance spaces: a 500-seat orchestral concert hall, a smaller recital hall, an organ studio, a 'black box' experimental room and the Eastside Jazz Club.

The technical challenges posed by these spaces were significant, particularly within the finite constraints of the site's relatively small footprint and the university's budget. Each of them required a different acoustic treatment to suit their size and intended programme of music, which in turn influenced all aspects of the design, necessitating an exceptional level of architectural, environmental and acoustic integration. The client is delighted with the quality of these spaces and the flexibility they provide both for public performances and the Conservatoire's day-to-day teaching and recording activities. Pride of place is given to the orchestral hall, where in common with the other venues and the foyer, a delicately detailed timber panel system, developed with the acoustic consultant, was adopted. Higher up, the corrugated timber

UNIVERSITY OF BIRMINGHAM INDOOR SPORTS CENTRE

Lifschutz Davidson Sandilands

CLIENT: UNIVERSITY OF BIRMINGHAM
LOCATION: BIRMINGHAM
PHOTOGRAPHY: HUFTON + CROW, PAUL RIDDLE

On a gateway site on the edge of the University's Edgbaston campus, the client's aspiration was not only for a state-of-the-art sports centre for students and staff, but a new building that would invite participation by the local community

MAKING THE ACTIVITIES inside as visible as possible was key, something usually at odds with the large volumes and inward-looking nature of typical sports spaces.

Taking advantage of the sloping site, the architects were able to organise the large component parts of the brief (50 metre pool, large multi-purpose hall, squash complex, fitness suites and car park) in a coherent, legible way without becoming over-bearing. A bronze-clad arch frames the main entrance and is extruded along the length of the site – an external marker of the centre's main axis of circulation that connects to the pool on one side and the multi-purpose hall on the other.

Pool and hall are distinguished externally by their brick façades, which tie them into the neighbouring student union building and the character of the campus's original brick nucleus. This simple choice gives the centre an immediate sense of place, avoiding the temptation to fall back on today's default sports centre palette of high-tech steel and glass. There is still plenty of glass, though, as well as the large-span structures required to cover the volumes, but these are simply handled and never allowed to dominate the main spaces.

The many smaller rooms (for changing, teaching, offices, and fitness suites) are deftly incorporated into the building's stepped section, which is also used to good effect to open up cross-views between spaces.

The building's civic role is celebrated externally by a portico flanking the pool, which marks the campus boundary and guides the visitor round to the main entrance. Within the tall entrance foyer a climbing wall immediately engages the eye, showcasing the building's activities. In a similar way the entrance café, placed strategically on the building's most prominent corner, looks onto the pool, so the building's social and sporting agendas are always visibly intertwined.

Since opening, the centre's membership from both university and town has surged, exceeding all expectations – a fitting recognition of the client's vision and the way it has been given form by the architects. The new centre provides a broad range of highly flexible and well-equipped spaces that can be adapted for different sports and public events; a level of adaptability that in other sports facilities can sometimes result in a dullness of character, but here it is achieved with memorable civic spirit.

UNIVERSITY OF ROEHAMPTON LIBRARY

Feilden Clegg Bradley Studios

CLIENT: UNIVERSITY OF ROEHAMPTON

LOCATION: LONDON, SW15

PHOTOGRAPHY: HUFTON + CROW

The new library at the University of Roehampton is a successful civic building, constructed with studious effort, that offers its users a number of delightful places to undertake library work

PART OF A wider masterplan to transform the entry to the complex, the building successfully holds a new soft water landscape to the east and creates a hard public realm to the west. Entry is naturally located to the south at the end of a boulevard on an axis with the primary entrance to the site.

The entrance informs the ground plane of the building, taking advantage of the sloping site and creating a loggia to the east with the library café, only open to library users to the north. Enjoying a high volume in the section with triple aspect, the journey down the internal staircase into the library is a joy.

The cross-section responds well to site with cellular spaces to the west shielding views of less-than-beautiful existing buildings, while the centre of the plan with the atria and the west façade are where, volumetrically and socially, the architectural experience is focused to great effect.

On entry the user is welcomed into one of two atria that define the parti along the length of the building. This specific atrium is two storeys high, offering a generosity in section that leads to a cleverly designed security sequence, with a shifted reception desk for both entry and exit.

The second atrium, where the wide main stair is located, offers a grand circulation experience as users move up and down the building. Light is welcomed into the heart of the plan and attention to detail is clear at the ends of the atria, where glazed balustrades are used to maintain views of the books in the shelving that matches down the length of each floor plate.

The Cartesian architecture is impressively reinforced through the structural and construction design; a strong grid runs through the building with acoustics, services, structure and structural columns working effectively with the rhythm of book storage and its relationship with the east façade – a success in its play of threshold both to the horizon and vertically to the sky, as seating, vestibules and double-height study spaces attract different user groups to the view and light within the piano nobile floors.

Externally these spaces aesthetically inform the geometry and depth of the façade, creating a deep skin within which users can work. The building sits comfortably with its neighbours, clad in similar brick and expressing its vertical section to the public landscape.

Internally, robust yet delightful precast concrete and oak linings are used with acoustic baffles that are reminiscent of the Yale Centre for British Art by Louis Kahn, as are the slightly tapered edges to the light portals at the top of the main atrium.

As Kahn said, a library starts by 'taking a book to light'. The new university library successfully meets this aim, creating many joyful places within a strict and meticulously constructed architecture, which succeeds in not only locating the individual within the building but also the individual within the wider campus.

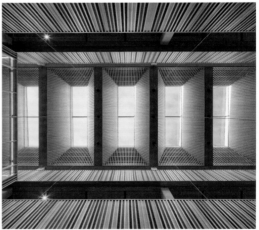

4

HOUSING & CARE

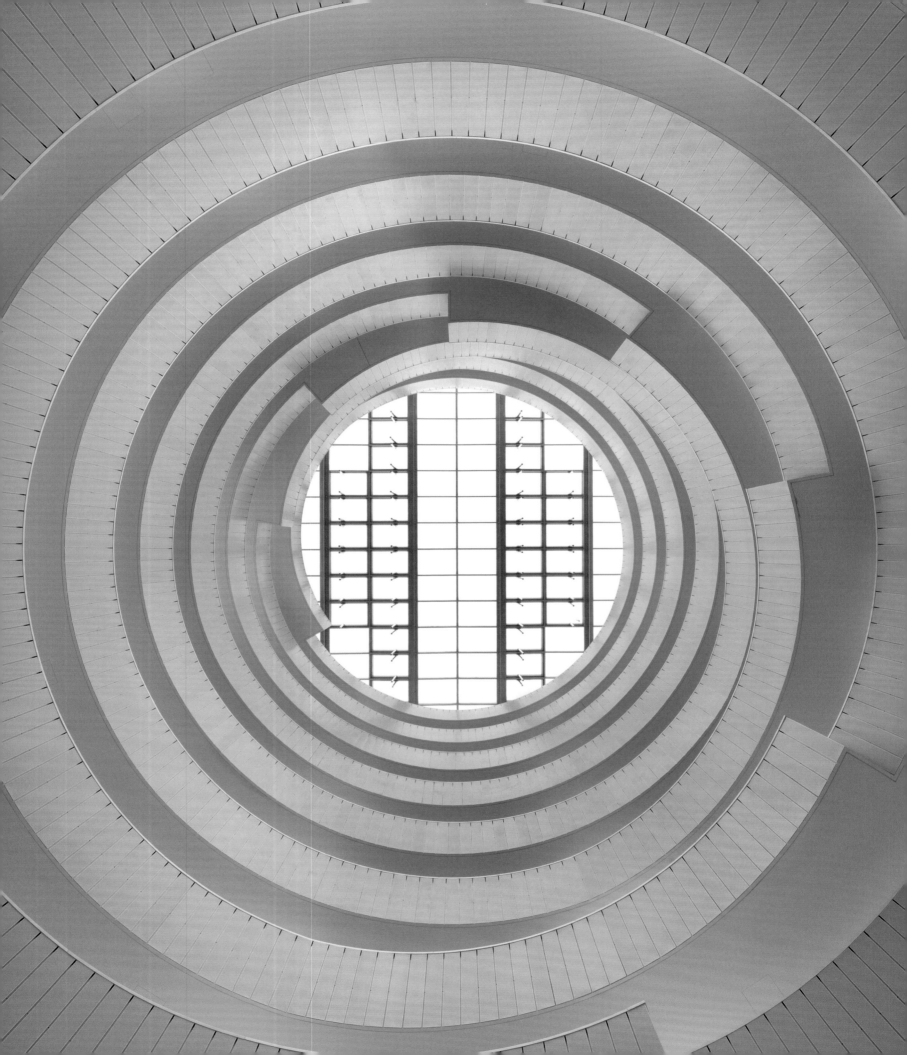

HOUSING & CARE

Even within the robust remits of housing, student accommodation and care homes, top architects are creating striking and impressive buildings

I think we judge housing differently to the way in which we might judge a cultural building. Housing has to be about its liveability, how it deals with private and public spaces, about the front and the back, about integrating social housing and private housing, about ensuring that different types of tenures co-exist alongside each other. Housing has a wider social remit; it has to fit into the city and connect with its infrastructure; it's the background to people's lives. It doesn't have to be an architectural set piece, but there needs to be longevity – you don't want to build something that's going to be demolished in 30 years' time. However, even within these constraints, some of these projects show that it's possible to build memorable buildings for housing.

I think this is an optimistic time for housing. More and more really good architects are designing these projects, and there have been numerous award winners in this category. On this list, Weston Street (a space-age series of apartments above an office space in Bermondsey) and 15 Clerkenwell Close (a six-storey building near Clerkenwell Green) are really interesting projects. They're both very different, but great examples of quite innovative ways to think about private housing. 15 Clerkenwell Close is quite an extraordinary building to come across. It uses an external curtain of structural stone to support the whole scheme, so it looks like a series of rough-hewn stones have been stacked up to support all of the flats – like some ancient medieval ruin.

Royal Albert Wharf Phase 1 in East London, and the King's Crescent Estate Phases 1 and 2 in King's Cross, are obviously larger-scale city projects, and are equally impressive in the way that they've dealt with public space and social housing, mixed with private housing. From the work that our architectural practice has done on similar inner-city projects, we can see how important that relationship is – hopefully you can't tell the different between the private housing and the social housing.

There's definitely a trend in housing to use brick, particularly in London. Concrete is a beautiful material but it is expensive. Brick is a more robust material, and urban housing needs to be robust. The two exceptions on this list are Riverlight in Nine Elms, near Battersea, and Gasholders in King's Cross. Both are in less gritty locations, and had budgets to use different materials. Riverlight is a high-density development by EPR Architects and Rogers Stirk Harbour, and it's in a prime riverside location. It's a similar idea to what RSH did at NEO Bankside developments, where they have angled the windows to let in the maximum amount of light, and to afford the most riverside views. Each building is a six-sided structure with an exposed steel frame, and it has social housing onsite, looking the same as the private housing.

Gasholders is a very striking structure. This building obviously used to be three drum-shaped gasholders from the 19th century, so that historic structure is still very visible. This is very high-end residential housing, very expensive and exclusive, but the design is impressive, filled with unusual and beautiful details. Structures that involve a change of use are always difficult – there is a very rigorous set of criteria and a constantly refining set of regulations that need to be obeyed – so it's great to see it done so well.

Five Acre Barn stands slightly outside from the other housing projects here. It's located near Aldeburgh in Suffolk, and the architect, Blee Halligan, has provided bed and breakfast accommodation in a long building with a zigzag roof, clad in shingles. It's very charming, and fits in with the local landscape.

With the expansion of higher education, there has definitely been a growth in student accommodation. And most of the purpose-built housing for students was pretty awful, to be honest – it's not a sector that has been particularly focused on design quality. It is unusual for student accommodation to get on an architectural design shortlist, so it's great that two of them have made it onto this list. Chadwick Hall at the University of Roehampton and Victoria Hall King's Cross, for students of the Aga Khan University, are both low-to-medium-rise schemes and they've both invested in high-quality materials.

When it comes to care centres, I think Maggie's has pioneered a new approach.

CONCRETE IS A BEAUTIFUL MATERIAL BUT IT IS EXPENSIVE. BRICK IS A MORE ROBUST MATERIAL, AND URBAN HOUSING NEEDS TO BE ROBUST

They have more than a dozen centres around the UK and, architecturally, they seem to have set the agenda, in a way, for end-of-life care. The principles that they've developed – less clinical, more domestic, more welcoming, with a calm and comfortable environment, very much tied to their local environment – have set a standard for these kind of projects. The Maggie's in Lanarkshire by Rogers Stirk Harbour + Partners won the Stirling Prize a couple of years ago, and the Maggie's Centre in Oldham is also a great design, using cross-laminated timber and set above a beautiful garden. You notice a similar feel to the St David's Hospice, New In-Patient Unit, in Newport, Gwent, which is also welcoming and warm.

FIVE ACRE BARN

Blee Halligan

CLIENT: FIVE ACRE BARN B+B
LOCATION: SUFFOLK
PHOTOGRAPHY: SARAH BLEE

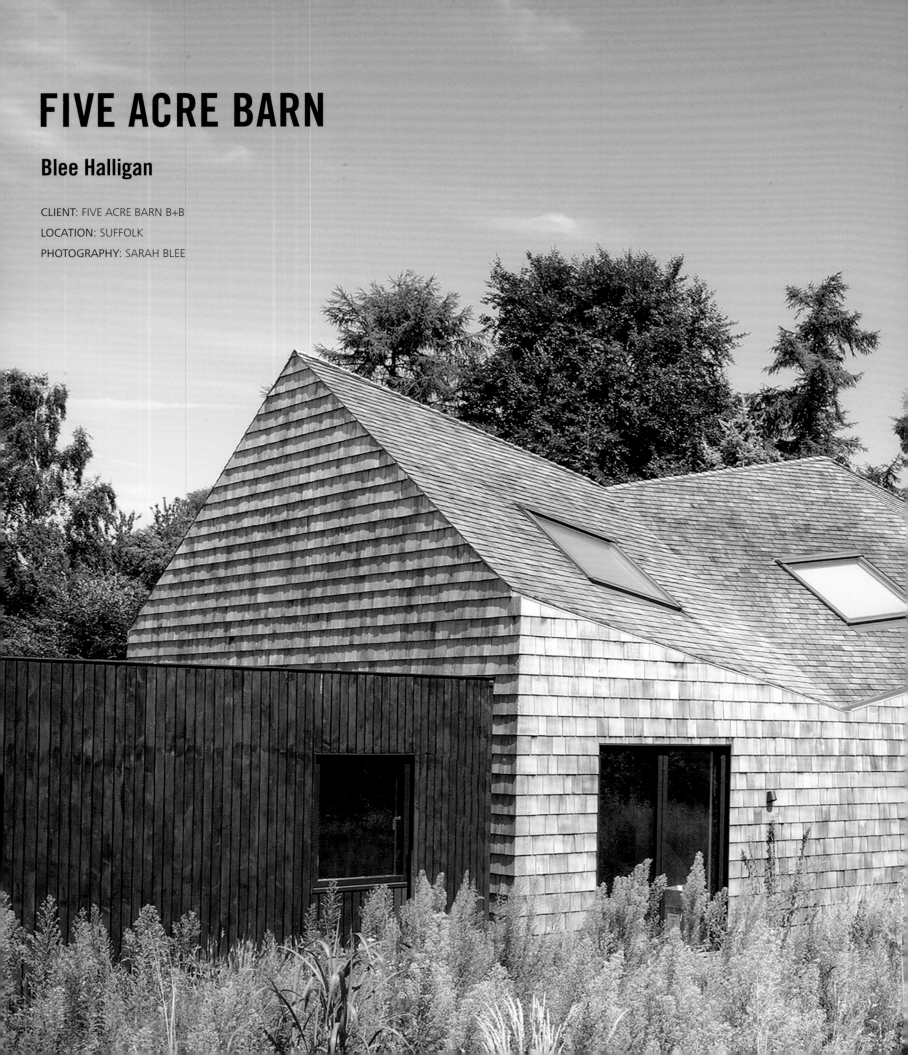

The Five Acre Barn is an original building form that is well suited to this new type of brief

THE SCHEME PROVIDES new-build bed and breakfast accommodation for five visitors (individuals, couples or families) who can choose to live and dine together for their stay, or use their room as a base to travel around this scenic area of Suffolk, with Aldeburgh being the nearest town to the site. The new building has a stepping, organic form, clad in shingles, that 'wriggles' among the trees in a mature garden (representing the 'five acres'). Each room is expressed in the roof form, and each room has its own timber deck projecting out into the landscape.

The new building is directly linked to a retained workshop building. This simple brick building has been repaired and enhanced in the most minimalist way – with the addition of an aluminium gutter, roof repairs and the odd new window – so that when you step inside, it is a surprise that it is a single volume comprising a stylish kitchen, dining room and lounge. Everywhere the finishes are minimal but the furniture (mid-century classics), pottery, prints, light fittings and so on, bring the style and purchasing power of Shoreditch to Suffolk.

What is most surprising and pleasing, given the quality of finishes and workmanship, is that this is largely a self-build project where the owners installed the cedar shingles, completed most of the joinery and decorations, and worked alongside the builder, Paul Ralph, every day on site. The scale and the budget are both modest, but this imaginative building punches well above its weight.

GASHOLDERS LONDON

WilkinsonEyre with Jonathan Tuckey Design

CLIENT: KING'S CROSS CENTRAL LIMITED PARTNERSHIP

LOCATION: LONDON, N1

PHOTOGRAPHY: JOHN STURROCK, PETER LANDERS

The industrial heritage of King's Cross is integral to its regeneration, and the triplet of Grade II listed cast-iron gasholders is a distinctive centrepiece

CONSTRUCTED IN 1867, these heavy industrial structures in their full restoration remain a dominant feature of the new skyline of King's Cross.

Sitting comfortably within these structures are the three residential drums, clad in a delicate and intricate aesthetic of steel and glass panels, with a veil of external shutters pierced in a pattern of circles to allow dappled light into the rooms. These create a homogenous yet dynamic skin, paying homage to the original drums that once sat in these gasholder guide frames. However, they also fulfil a functional and environmental requirement for modern living. The façade design addresses the challenges of privacy, solar shading and window dressing while simultaneously highlighting the industrial character of the gasholders.

The architect approached the configuration of the three interlocking drums to create a fourth central drum-shaped courtyard, which is open and theatrical, with the conglomeration of the gasholder structures becoming tougher.

As a counterpoint to the external structure, the interior is based on the intrinsic aesthetics and mechanics of a watch. The brass linings in the polished floor, balustrade design and custom-designed door handles all reinforce this crafted approach to detail, and are reminiscent of Scarpa's instinctive designs, combining base materials with precious ones. A brass lining to the vertical edge of the external shutters extends this approach onto the façade.

The residential drums are set at differing heights to suggest the historic movement of the gasholders, and each one with its own central atrium floods light down into the heart of the structure and into the apartments through diffused glass screens. The circular walkways and light-

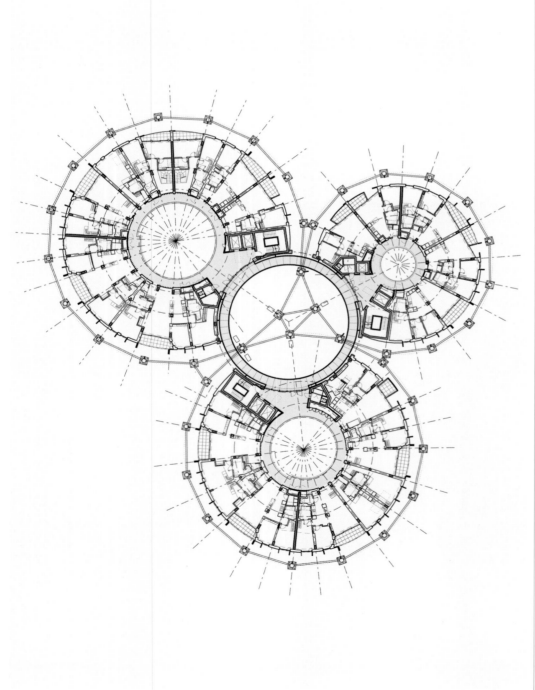

reflective surfaces create a 'Guggenheim' feel to encourage interaction with neighbours and other residents.

The integral design of the wayfinding throughout the development, with signage embossed into the textured concrete panels, is achieved with great intelligence. This considered approach to the design is also evident within the apartments, with a take on boutique hotels where the detail of the fixtures and fittings is meticulous and custom-made. The layouts of the pie-shaped apartments are well-planned, embracing the concept of a radial arrangement to benefit from expansive views and daylight.

The provision of a spa, gym, roof garden, cinema and business lounge all add to a modern lifestyle offer. The client is discovering that the demographic of residents is proving to be older than expected, with an appreciation for the quality of detail and the way the apartments combine functionality with innovative technologies.

Gasholders London is a successful marriage of old and new, sensitively handling the needs of modern 21st-century living and celebrating the most beautiful industrial structures in the renaissance of King's Cross.

KINGS CRESCENT ESTATE PHASES 1 AND 2

Karakusevic Carson Architects and Henley Halebrown

CLIENT: LONDON BOROUGH OF HACKNEY

LOCATION: LONDON

PHOTOGRAPHY: JIM STEPHENSON, PETER LANDERS, TIM CROCKER, NICK KANE

The original Kings Crescent Estate had been half-demolished in 2000 and the remaining community have lived with the resulting wasteland until now

INSTEAD OF THE usual demolition and rebuild model for large-scale estate regeneration, this project shows that community combined with local authority-led development can be a way forward to create a robust model for new and refurbished housing.

By upgrading the existing housing (with large balconies, winter gardens and garages) and converting it into new flats, the existing residents were very much engaged with the estate development, which allowed them to remain in their homes throughout the development. The masterplan created new connections and permeable spaces: three courtyards, each with a very different emphasis, from contemplation to play and a gardening club, while an intelligently furnished play street helps community integration in creating a new public space.

Two architectural practices, Karakusevic Carson Architects and Henley Halebrown, working closely together, have successfully allowed more variety in the build. This project has resulted from a strong collaboration between the client (the London Borough of Hackney), and the architects, and stands as an example of what can be achieved in future developments within the borough and beyond.

The three new brick-clad blocks vary in height from five to 12 storeys, and interact well with the park and local streets, creating a family of buildings. Brick, concrete, steel and timber provide a simple

palette for the estate. The brickwork contains subtle Art Deco detailing, while timber is used on the balconies and in the generous lobbies. The dual-aspect entrances are light and airy, allowing views through to courtyards and shared amenities, and offering a sense of delight and intrigue. The hardwood timber-framed shop fronts sit well at street level.

This is a well-considered residential scheme that has repaired the previously desolate areas and helped to form a sense of community and ownership. A tenure-blind scheme has reconnected the estate with the outside world and engaged the residents throughout the transformation of their estate.

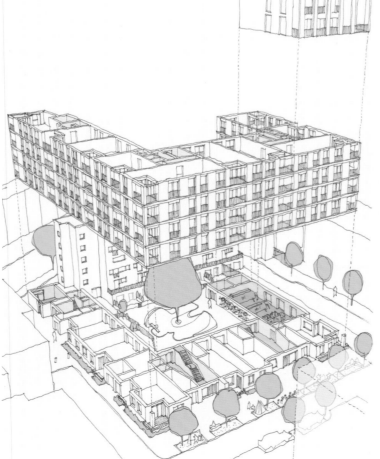

VICTORIA HALL KING'S CROSS

Stanton Williams

CLIENT: ARGENT (KING'S CROSS) LTD ACTING ON BEHALF OF KING'S CROSS
CENTRAL LIMITED PARTNERSHIP / AGA KHAN DEVELOPMENT NETWORK
LOCATION: LONDON, N1C
PHOTOGRAPHY: HUFTON + CROW

As part of the King's Cross regeneration, Victoria Hall is a cultural identity for the graduate students of the Aga Khan University

THE ARCHITECT HAS raised the bar for the design quality of student residences, where the immaculate detailing and high-quality, natural finishes convey a sense of permanence as well as referencing both the adobe architecture of the Middle East and the industrial heritage of King's Cross.

The crafted detailing of the internal spaces combines furniture with surfaces where the carved oak benches and warm limestone floors come together beautifully. Meanwhile, the fixed and bespoke designed furniture in the bedrooms and living areas adds a layer of refinement, making the spaces feel generous and graceful.

The arrangement, orientation and massing of the scheme addresses the awkwardness of the site very well, in particular its edge to the elevated railway line and flanked boundaries to the emerging terrace of buildings. The simple organisation of the plan minimises north-facing bedrooms overlooking the railway and carves out the southern perimeter to maximise its frontage for the bedrooms.

You are welcomed by a recessed volume in the ground floor plinth, which cunningly conceals the cycle entrance while inviting you through to the reception. The sequence of spaces from the timber panelled reception up to the courtyard works very well, creating opportunities to rest, meet and dwell with other fellow students. At all times, you experience the generosity of natural light and volume together, with views across into communal areas through the large expanse of delicate glazed walls.

At the heart and on the top of the building are contemplative south-facing gardens, demonstrating influences from Alhambra and Morocco. Both are eloquently fitted out to offer a different yet tranquil haven amidst the pulsating surroundings of King's Cross.

The monolithic approach to the form is echoed in the use of a single material for the façade, vents and balconies, using irregular brickwork. With the vent panels and balcony furniture situated behind this perforated brickwork, the exterior appears calm and serious while the interior spaces are dappled with light.

All in all, the effort in detailing and setting out components to achieve perfection has delivered an effortless piece of architecture that fosters a sense of community and home.

15 CLERKENWELL CLOSE

Amin Taha + Groupwork

CLIENT: 15CC
LOCATION: LONDON, EC1
PHOTOGRAPHY: TIM SOAR

The unassuming name of 15 Clerkenwell Close belies the astonishing architectural triumph that dwells at that simple address, occupying a plot of land that's a stone's throw from Clerkenwell Green

THE SEVEN-STOREY building is the architect's own development, comprising one or two flats per floor, a double-height architect's studio at basement and ground level, and the architect's home on the top floor.

To hear the architect talk about the project, including a lengthy analysis of the history of the site dating back to an eleventh-century Norman abbey, it becomes clear that the thoroughness and care that have gone into every thought and every inch of the project crossed the border of obsession very early in the process. The result is a truly bespoke, handcrafted work of art, but one that has a grace and balance – suggesting that the obsession was harnessed rather than letting the madness in.

The development occupies the extent of the site, appearing to have the proportions of a cube, with the façade divided into squares. A pathway alongside leads to a tiny, delightful, urban pebble garden, belonging to the council, but landscaped and maintained by the architect client. It's just one of many aspects of this story where an unusual and surprising decision has led to a sparkling outcome, for both the building's occupants and the public.

The façade is formed from limestone structural columns and beams set back from, but structurally connected to, the building envelope with a variety of finishes: smooth, rough, drilled, straight from the quarry. The 'fallen' column folly, with decorative carving nods to the handcrafted workmanship of the material, indicates the richness of the narrative and joy experienced throughout the project.

Entering the building over the pebbled floor, dodging the glass walk on roof lights and stepping onto the architecture studio's bridge

feels like you have stepped into a void suspended between the basement well below and the heavy mass of the building floating above, surrounded by the neighbouring party walls, exposed and celebrated. With the floating glass meeting room balanced on an L-beam, and the folding raw metal stair with impossible handrail angularly leading down to the studio space below; all of these components sit together with different materials and characters, but are connected by a similar attitude to simplicity, rawness and expression of the materials and junctions.

The residential development is anything but standard, and has a touch of childlike playfulness in the inventiveness of the various communal elements. The glass lift with innovative fire strategy replacing lobbies, the metal grille stairwell, the rooftop tree and reed garden are all unique experimentations challenging the obvious and the norm. The entrance corridor bridges through the studio like it might in a child's imagination, a timber-clad tunnel leading to a postbox wall that unexpectedly swings back to reveal the possibility of a secret concierge's office.

The flats themselves are all concrete and wood with polished floors, exposed ceilings, and oak doors and walls sliding and slotting, folding and swinging together in a complex matrix of patterns to open up or shut down different spaces like a complex puzzle. Each room leads into one another with traditional doorways, but also with sliding walls to allow a route around the façade. Everything is bespoke, every detail is cared for and every junction thought through, with everything built to an impeccable finish.

Brave, ambitious and highly innovative, the 15 Clerkenwell Close project has demonstrated that risk-taking can pay off, resulting in a truly imaginative, intriguing and astonishing work of architecture.

ROYAL ALBERT WHARF PHASE 1

Maccreanor Lavington Architects

CLIENT: NOTTING HILL HOUSING GROUP
LOCATION: LONDON, E16
PHOTOGRAPHY: TIM CROCKER

A new housing scheme which creates a new community in the Albert Basin at the east end of the Royal Albert Dock

THE TENURE INCLUDES shared ownership, affordable rent, private rented sector housing and market sale.

The project deals with flood risk by providing a highly useful hobby room at ground level which allows bikes, luggage and other occasionally used items to be stored easily and out of the way from actual living space. Direct access to the street is provided to avoid carrying these items through the home.

The buildings are embellished with a rich brick cladding with distinctive colours identifying individual buildings. This is articulated with a combination of glazed brick spandrel panels and coloured precast concrete string courses and copings. The palette of materials is friendly and timeless.

Attention is paid to bin stores and plant room access doors with patterned metalwork as well as the storage of wheelie bins, which are kept out of sight but allowed easy access.

Windows are placed at the end of communal corridors and draw you towards them, giving light and a sense of location. The homes themselves have large windows, allowing light to flood in and provide large useful spaces.

The central courtyards within the blocks are a good scale. They provide private outdoor space to ground floor flats, views from balconies onto the basin, children's play areas and a green space. Meanwhile, double-height community spaces are located on the corners of the blocks to provide life and vibrancy for this new waterside community.

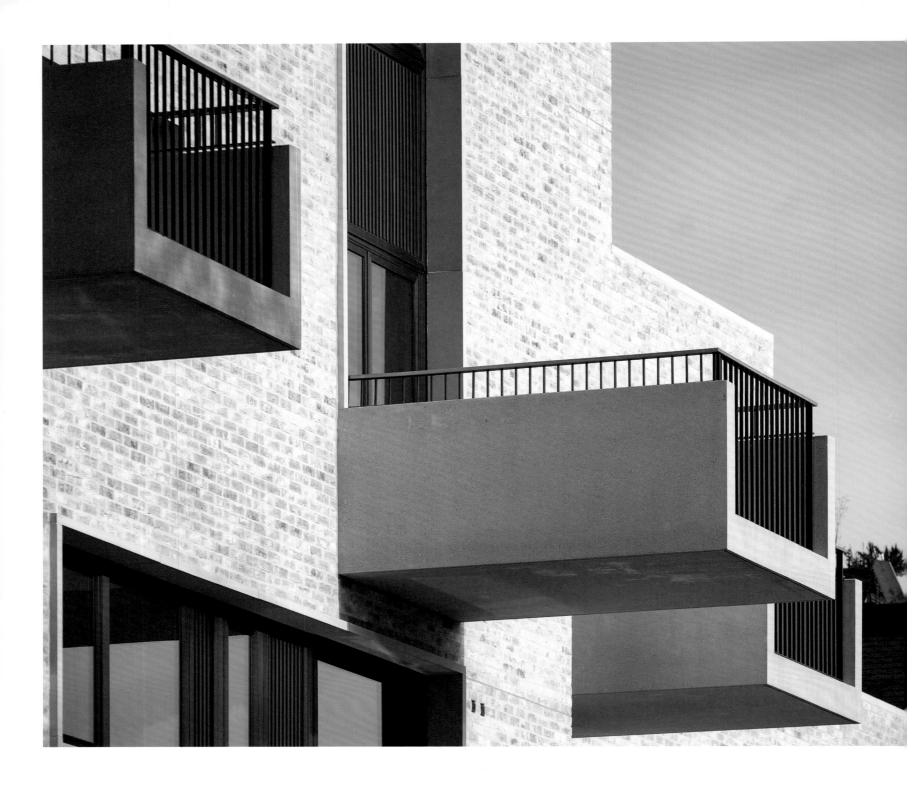

WESTON STREET

Allford Hall Monaghan Morris

CLIENT: SOLIDSPACE
LOCATION: LONDON, SE1
PHOTOGRAPHY: TIM SOAR

ARRANGED IN TWO staggered blocks with a stair and lift core running up the middle of each cluster, the split-section, dual-aspect apartments benefit from north and south light. The scheme uses the Solidspace model.

These are impeccably crafted modern homes. A tactile choice of materials has been used, coupled with beautiful interior detailing. The exposed concrete feels warm, welcoming and friendly with the timber interior linings of oak or walnut. The concrete has been poured in sections and cast using shutters of rough-sawn Douglas fir, giving a board-marked finish.

Large picture windows are part of all external walls, allowing plenty of light in and views out. Blinds are built into the windows. There are storage cupboards to store the everyday items of modern life like the ironing board as well as built-in joinery items like a bookcase.

The length of the balconies allow for the occupant to move away from the building to look back at it and, in doing so, they provide additional amenity space. The interlocking volumes of the apartments are expressed through large L- or T-shaped windows, set into deep reveals.

On the ground floor, office space covers the southern part of the building footprint, with a smaller meeting room and ancillary spaces tucked into the northern part of the plan. The office is self-finished in board-marked concrete.

This project has a sense of fun, providing an alternative model for fluid space living across split levels for the modern home.

This housing scheme comprises eight apartments of two or three bedrooms above a ground floor office space

CHADWICK HALL

Henley Halebrown

CLIENT: UNIVERSITY OF ROEHAMPTON

LOCATION: LONDON, SW15

PHOTOGRAPHY: DAVID GRANDORGE, NICK KANE

The scheme is set in the grounds of the Georgian Grade II* listed Downshire House which itself borders on London County Council's Alton West Estate (Grade II* listed)

THE BRIEF SOUGHT 210 en-suite student bedrooms. These are provided in three new buildings. Each employs a distinct plan type – two are villas, the third is a modernist pinwheel plan. Two are paired around an existing historic sunken garden. The third lies on an axis with the sunken garden to the south of Downshire House, completing an ensemble with the house that creates a theatre for the students' social life.

This is a good example of timeless architecture. It is inspiring while remaining simple. The scheme's success is also based on a skilful masterplan with sensitive arrangement of the blocks within the landscape, existing listed building and the restored sunken garden. The concept is a nod both to Georgian architecture as well as to a modernist block of flats to the north-west boundary of the

site. The design becomes a backdrop for the listed building and the sunken garden. It gives them a sense of importance and provides a setting for social gathering.

The main materials are limited to a dark red-brown brick and precast concrete, with a darker red brick which both relates to the listed building and yet remains subservient. The tall windows in all the blocks are for the bedrooms, with wider ones for communal areas. The only exception is the large bay window, which attempts to respond to the bay window of the listed building. The low cost of the building is not at all reflected in the external appearance of the scheme.

The panel felt that the architects managed to create a welcoming and calm space by careful masterplanning, responding in turn to the street and the listed building structures as well as the wider landscape and the modernist building on the perimeter of the site.

RIVERLIGHT

Rogers Stirk Harbour + Partners with EPR Architects

CLIENT: ST JAMES GROUP
LOCATION: LONDON, SW11
PHOTOGRAPHY: JOAS SOUZA, ANTHONY COLEMAN

Aptly named, this series of dense housing fingers responds to its impressive site by cleverly manipulating its mass and circulation to offer daylight and views of the river to all of its residents

THE BOLD DIAGRAM and structural system also offers generous public realm to all those who walk along the Thames.

Six narrow blocks, orientated north/south, provide east- or west-facing units that line linear gardens or commercial squares; landscapes that provide the public and residents views to the river. The spaces created are punctuated with organic islands of greenery and threaded with water features that bring life and a soothing acoustic.

The north/south orientation of these gardens creates permeability to the river edge for residents and allows for sun penetration to the southern bank of the river; cantilevers here add further generosity to this edge, and its opposite street edge, encouraging activity throughout the day as people enjoy the retail, commercial, and food and beverage offerings at ground level. The fingers reduce in height to the west as a contextual nod to Battersea Power Station further along the river.

Occupants of larger maisonettes enjoy the ground plane with their own external private gardens; these people who live above the vertical circulation are brought outside of the building skin, and are offered dynamic expansive views of the landscapes, the city and the river below. This singular move is extremely successful in creating a sense of place and identity for the individuals who live here.

The modular nature of the housing within a tight and aesthetically articulated construction allows for variety across the floor plate by introducing a wide solid external panel against which internal partitions can be planted. The canted balconies in between offer external amenity space that is both efficient but also 'enclosed', not being exposed on the perceived 'outside' of the building. These are places where residents can enjoy fresh air and views but are also offered an engaging dilution of the threshold from the inside.

Expressed structural members bring dexterity and lightness to the long façades and allow a reading of the buildings' forces from ground props to the switched structure of the gull-wing roofs. Colour brings further vibrancy to elevations of double-storey expressive concrete, diagonal steels and lightweight balconies.

As a way of developing mass housing on a riverside site to the south, this series of buildings is exceptional for both residents and the public. For its part it offers bright sunlit space for all, both externally and internally, and in its effortless construction it offers beautiful reflection and a lightness of touch and vibrant colour to this important transition site on the edge of the Battersea Power Station regeneration.

ST DAVID'S HOSPICE, NEW IN-PATIENT UNIT

KKE Architects

CLIENT: ST DAVID'S HOSPICE CARE

LOCATION: WALES

PHOTOGRAPHY: STILLVIEW PHOTOGRAPHY, STÅLE ERIKSEN

THE NEW BUILDING owes much of its special quality to unusually insightful clients. Their brief for the new building has applied evidence gathered in the operation of the charity's other centres and awareness of international best practice. Lessons learned have been applied in the clinical and operational aspects but also, most importantly, in the nature of the ideal aesthetic environment for end-of-life care.

Those of us who attend on a family member during their last days will not forget the character of their surroundings at such times; surroundings that are far too often both chaotic and austere. For those who have reason to visit St David's

The 15-bed in-patient hospice is a development of the original 2013 Day Hospice, itself a shortlisted project

Hospice the experience is very different and, in so far as it is possible at such a time, in many ways really uplifting.

Nothing matters more to the patient than the feelings of the family that they leave behind, so it follows that the focus of design should be on the experience of visitors as much, if not more, than on the patients themselves.

The hospice is beautifully calm and serene. It achieves an air of spirituality while avoiding any implication of judgemental sanctity. The colours and materials are restrained: a tightly controlled palette of warm natural tones. The consistency is thoughtful and deliberate, a specific requirement of the client that patients and visitors should not be distracted by any implied differentiation between occupants.

Spaces for withdrawal and contemplation follow the secular spiritual approach. Natural materials are used contrary to sterile clinical convention. Hygiene control may require more effort, but the environmental aesthetic benefits take precedence over any added operational burden.

The patients' rooms have a gentle domestic character. Clinical fixtures are unobtrusive. Furniture and built-in fittings are refined, smoothly co-ordinated and well constructed. Careful consideration has been applied to every element; nothing is left to irritate or to jar the senses. For such a complex facility this level of design control is a terrific achievement.

MAGGIE'S OLDHAM

dRMM

CLIENT: MAGGIE'S
LOCATION: OLDHAM
PHOTOGRAPHY: TONY BARWELL, ALEX DE RIJKE, JASMIN SOHI

**This is an exquisite building created with loving care.
It is a delight to the senses, yet economical, efficient and highly sustainable**

THE CLIENT AND users adore the building, which enables them to work in ways they had not anticipated – even after such a successful catalogue of Maggie's centres. It is a great credit to both client and architect that the trusting relationship and intense commitment have allowed such a fresh reinvention of this typology.

The site is well chosen and deftly used, turning a redundant set of retaining walls into an open and inviting walled garden, with a looseness and generosity that succeeds in inviting a diverse range of hospital users to spend time there. The spaces under the building successfully achieve a credible and delightful undercroft garden – a rare achievement.

Perched above the garden on slender legs is a timber box reached across a bridge. Even on a rainy grey day, entering the building is a delight to the senses, the bright yellow floor and sinuous glazed courtyard transporting the visitor to sunnier exotic places. The plan feels loose and free-flowing but is cleverly created to give privacy and intimacy for each of the many overlapping functions – the inviting in, the intimate chats and group support. Maggie's have long referenced the domestic and the sense of home, but here that home is aspirational and escapist in the best sense – an optimistic vision of living, up in the trees, with long views of landscape. It is positive, life-affirming and joyous.

Meticulous craft and thoughtful detailing permeate the scheme, including both intelligent inventive workings of modern methods of construction and vigorous use of traditional technique. The building exploits the full potential of cross-laminated timber as structure and finish, the new technology of heat-treated tulipwood, and even uses offcuts to create soffits and furniture, such as the large circular table, like a huge cotton reel turned on an enormous lathe. Wooden handles help the sensitised skin of patients undergoing treatment.

Even the familiar tropes of flexibility and hospital care are elevated to a new level; a large reversible curtain is used to create a sheltered space, its silver lining and round windows completely transforming the space and creating a wholly new atmosphere.

5

OFFICES & WORKSPACES

OFFICES & WORKSPACES

Judging by this year's awards, the best workspaces and offices are flexible, multi-functional, community-conscious public spaces that often hark back to their industrial roots

I would argue that the open-plan office has been around since at least 1939, when Frank Lloyd Wright completed the Johnson Wax headquarters in Wisconsin. He saw it as a forest open to the sky, with the columns supporting the roof like tree canopies. Since then the layouts of offices and other workspaces have become less formal within an open-plan arrangement. The office building is now more a blank canvas; a space where tenants can build communities. People have less desk permanence, but there are more of a range of working environments available in any one building.

Flexibility is absolutely crucial. A workspace has to be robust. When we were working on the BBC Media Village in White City in 2000, we had to address one of the issues that the BBC had suffered in the 1990s,

which was one of "churn". The existing space that they had wasn't flexible enough for changing programmes and changing groups. So it is important that spaces are multi-functional and adaptable. Today's workplaces need open-plan spaces, smaller rooms for private conversations, but bigger ones too for congregating and social events.

Invariably, a single building will often have different tenants with different requirements. Even at the Leadenhall Building, for instance, you might have traditional offices for the insurance industry on one floor, and then there is Rogers Stirk Harbour on another floor, making very different use of the space. But none undermine the clarity and success of the original building.

Repurposing is becoming a more important aspect of workplace design. The Albert Works in Sheffield, for instance, negotiates the reuse of an existing building – four derelict redbrick warehouses that date back to the Victorian era – and, internally, provides several different types of space. It is an exemplar for the reuse of our industrial past. Victorian warehouses, with their often large floorplates and voluminous interiors, make for inspiring workspaces – much like Frank Lloyd Wright's Johnson Wax. I guess that idea of repurposing has been with us since at least the 1970s, and the debate in

FLEXIBILITY IS ABSOLUTELY CRUCIAL. A WORKSPACE HAS TO BE ROBUST

the UK about the retention of historic buildings. Covent Garden Market was an early example, in the 1970s. It's definitely how best to engage with the city, and it's the sensible thing to do – economically, culturally and environmentally. These buildings are deep in the memories of many people, and bringing them back to life is beneficial to the entire community.

There is today an appreciation, a joy, about the industrial quality and aesthetic. Repurposed industrial buildings often embrace elements from their productive past. We used to talk about "warehouses for work", and a lot of these new buildings

have that sense of industrial flexibility. A frequent downside is that it is sometimes difficult to maintain high environmental standards with repurposed buildings. Insulation standards, for instance, can be hard to achieve. But all of these offices have been assessed by BREEAM (Building Research Establishment Environmental Assessment Method) and all have been graded either "very good" or above.

Increasingly, architects are doing more with less. Many of these buildings will have been stripped back to the shell and core and then the tenants may or may not put ceilings in. There is more lighting variety – gone are the days of acres of bland, consistent strip lighting – you're likely to get different shades of light throughout a building. There's also a restraint about materials. At the White Collar Factory, a 16-storey building near

Old Street, a lot of the wall finishes are both structural and aesthetic. So there is a sense that one can make a building robust without needing to add finishing layers on the building. 53 Great Suffolk Street – a repurposed Victorian warehouse in Bermondsey – has extensive exposed brickwork, which is part of the structure. Incorporating it can minimise the cost, but also add richness and character.

At the Department Store, which repurposes an old shop in Brixton, the building has been stripped back to its frame, internally, and the space is fitted out with the mechanical engineering and equipment that has been reinstalled into the frame. It is a re-imagination of the industrial, and people are enjoying that.

Office buildings are also embracing more of a mix. Most of these workspaces incorporate retail space; some will have

bars and restaurants. R7 has a cinema entered through the reception space, with plans for a future gym and a restaurant in the reception. The Leadenhall Building, despite high security concerns, has public space all around it. Bloomberg will have a museum space, along with restaurants and bars – with most of those tenants chosen by the staff of Bloomberg. White Collar Factory has a public café in its reception. All of these buildings have committed to making a contribution to their context, which makes them attractive to people who are buying the space and people who live around them. This is definitely true of the Department Store, which is a huge commitment to regeneration in that area. The public-facing spaces are very important. It demonstrates that the best offices and workspaces face outwards to engage with that local community.

ALBERT WORKS

Cartwright Pickard

CLIENT: CITY ESTATES
LOCATION: SHEFFIELD
PHOTOGRAPHY: TOM KAHLER

Located within the Cultural Industries Quarter Conservation Area of Sheffield, this project brings back into use four virtually derelict warehouse buildings

THE EXISTING PERIMETER buildings have been carefully refurbished with a new courtyard infill, providing a double-height space and integrated core. New elements are crisp and modern insertions that create flexible workspace for Jaywing, a Sheffield-based creative marketing agency. The project 'speaks' Sheffield with confidence.

Cartwright Pickard have skilfully negotiated a clever design which seeks to balance the potentially conflicting demands of landlord and tenant. Using Construction Management Procurement allowed the developer client and end user to be jointly involved in key decision-making regarding the design strategies, M+E systems, fitted furniture and finishes.

The scheme is sympathetic to its context in reuse of existing buildings, but bold and clear interventions provide impact. Externally anodised aluminium cladding marks the infill elevation to Matilda Street. Internally exposed concrete and brickwork provides thermal mass, which assists the environmental performance of the space. The courtyard infill virtually doubles the usable space and creates a new heart for the office accommodation.

The space is wonderfully lit by north lights and provides a generous and calm working environment. Furniture and finishes are co-ordinated with a fine attention to detail throughout.

R7, KING'S CROSS

Morris+Company with Weedon Architects

CLIENT: ARGENT LLP
LOCATION: LONDON, N1C
PHOTOGRAPHY: JACK HOBHOUSE

The colourful backdrop to the Granary Building in the King's Cross regeneration programme is R7 – the next generation of workplace

ITS STRIKING AND somewhat eccentric presence on a quiet street is by virtue of its colour and stepped form. The form has been established by working within the prescriptive parameters of the outline approval and in doing so, the architect has successfully maximised the opportunity.

The attempt to break down this massing through a series of set-backs and recesses creates south-facing terraces or gardens on each level, which benefit from views across the city. This sequence and laudable provision of outdoor spaces provides a sculptural interest and character to the building, often rare in corporate office buildings.

The two distinct shades of satin pink to the metal finned façade helps to split the block into two, with one part being grounded by an exposed concrete colonnade. Everything on this building feels bespoke and colour matched to the 'pink' façade, from the suspended lights in the colonnade to the paved flags on the terraces. It is a testament to the architect's attention to detail and drive to make this project something very special and original.

The architect has strived to challenge the norm for office architecture, and the ground floor experience is no exception. With its range of mixed uses including a restaurant, cocktail bar and boutique cinema, it is growing into a welcoming public foyer where one wants to spend time. The sincerity in the 'stripped back' internal finishes with the exposed concrete structure is a delightful contrast to the crisp exterior, also offering flexibility and minimising abortive costs for tenant fit-outs.

The architect's awareness to prioritise spending where it matters is evident in the design quality of the public spaces and amenities – money spent wisely. The building tackles the problem of evolving workspaces well, allowing flexible fit-outs – particularly between floors, with 'soft spots' for connecting stairs and spaces.

R7 pushes boundaries and may represent the next generation of workspace, and is already attracting businesses from the more established financial districts of London.

BLOOMBERG, LONDON

Foster + Partners

CLIENT: BLOOMBERG LP
LOCATION: LONDON, EC4
PHOTOGRAPHY: NIGEL YOUNG/FOSTER + PARTNERS,
AARON HARGREAVES/FOSTER + PARTNERS

Occupying a whole block within the City of London, this office building can house all of Bloomberg's employees under one roof for the first time

EXTERNALLY THE BUILDING incorporates a covered walkway all round its perimeter, which represents a level of generosity towards the city. There is also a new street created, carving the building into two blocks connected by bridges. Commercial units for restaurants are arranged at ground level. There is an external undulation in plan, described by the architect as an expression of the movement around the building. Upon entering the building and encountering some understandably very tight security, one moves through an architectural procession to the lifts. This procession includes 'the vortex', which is an art piece, one of several throughout the scheme. The lifts – specially designed – take you to a mid-level floor where the main concourse and café space is located. Desks and workspaces are then distributed in clusters accessible from a winding curved ramp, which curls through the building linking the various levels.

Internally, the process of moving through the architectural procession and upwards in the lifts creates a completely immersive environment. The concourse level is very vibrant, buzzing with activity and isolated from its surroundings. There's a sense of Willy Wonka about the space, and it is here where the real success of the project starts to emerge. Everywhere you look there is an inventive detail – from the bespoke folded aluminium ceiling 'roses' to the magnetic

floorboards. The aim of the building was to avoid standard office space, and it achieves that aim.

Overall the project is a tour-de-force; this is the opposite of a quiet understated building. In fact the multiplicity of invention at numerous levels is carried through with such conviction that you cannot fail to be impressed by it.

THE LEADENHALL BUILDING

Rogers Stirk Harbour + Partners

CLIENT: BRITISH LAND

LOCATION: LONDON, EC3

PHOTOGRAPHY: JAMES NEWMAN, RICHARD BYRANT BRITISH LAND/OXFORD PROPERTIES,

PETER SHANNON ROGERS STIRK HARBOUR + PARTNERS, PAUL RAFTERY

This new 50-storey skyscraper in the City of London is a neighbour to the iconic Lloyd's building by the same practice

ITS ALREADY FAMOUS slanted 'cheesegrater' form responds to client British Land's desire to be able to offer their own diverse clients office spaces of different floor areas – which diminish in size as the building rises – and the demand from planners to preserve key historic views of St Paul's Cathedral, particularly from Fleet Street. It is one of the more striking and elegant towers to have been added to the City's jumbled skyline in recent years.

The simplicity of the structural geometry in response to the brief is intriguing. Instead of a central core, the building has a full perimeter braced tube, which is visible as a giant, bold, steel exoskeleton on three sides, giving a visceral sense of the building's balancing act. The front façade glazes this over in a huge, straight, slick shimmering sweep from floor to sky, creating a dramatic contrast.

At the theatrical rear, all lifts and toilets are choreographed into a circulation and servicing core at the rear, again glazed. This creates a constant intricate dance of lifts of different colours and sizes and their inhabitants, rising and falling, filling and emptying. Functional necessity becomes something beautiful to watch – almost like a children's storybook of How A Building Works – and, again, contrasts with the slick front that is achieved with a seamless conviction.

The public space beneath means the building's lower potential seven storeys of its exoskeleton remain unbuilt, allowing the giant metal supporting 'legs' to create and enclose a canopied void. From that public space, escalators soar up to the offices above, where you really appreciate their scale and strength. This is not just an empty gesture, but accommodates a number of shops and cafés around its edges, within the structure, and so adds genuine life and additional pavement to the street as people criss-cross through it. Again, this feels quite theatrical. A new north/south route is also provided.

As a response to its surrounding townscape, it was decided to align the canopy over this void. With the height of the Lutyens building next door, it is a simple additional gesture that helps the Leadenhall building to have some kind of nodding respectful relationship with the older city streets beneath.

WHITE COLLAR FACTORY

Allford Hall Monaghan Morris

CLIENT: DERWENT LONDON
LOCATION: LONDON, EC1
PHOTOGRAPHY: TIM SOAR

The White Collar Factory is a new-build reinvention of a refurbished office typology

THE DEVELOPMENT FOLLOWED the completion of an eight-year-long research project by the architects and the client to investigate why refurbished Victorian industrial buildings often prove more popular to tenants than the modern-day, new-build equivalent. The outcome is an exemplary development full of quality materials, finishes, details and playfulness, alongside public and community-spirited generosity, innovation and experimentation (plus lots of lovely concrete).

The site strategy includes the creation of two new pedestrian streets through the site, broadening into a little square with a few trees and walk-on glass lights with views down to the unusual, cavernous basement – a space that was deliberately created to be programme-less to allow for the opportunity of accidental occupation. Six buildings are introduced on the site around the public space, including the retention and refurbishment of two historically decent corner buildings that help embed the development into the existing context. The buildings house a combination of offices, studios, incubator space, restaurants and apartments. The public permeability and integration of the scheme into the local narrow passage character should be commended.

The centrepiece is the 16-storey block fronting Old Street roundabout that has the architect's trademark excellent handling of board-marked concrete at its base.

Entering the public, double-to-treble-height concrete space at pavement level, one would be forgiven for thinking you had entered a high-end modern art gallery. The generous reception area, full of slack space, leads you around to a raised public café up a few terraced steps, encouraging people to perch and pause.

Following the results of the research project, the floor-to-ceilings heights are around 500 mm taller than standard, sacrificing the equivalent of two to three standard-height floors within the massing. The office space is naturally ventilated with opening windows behind grilles, the concrete provides thermal mass and carries the servicing, the public are encouraged into the ground floor space/café – overlapping the office life with the street life – and a Shoreditch-esque communal bar is located on the roof that is exclusively available for every tenant to use three times a year to help promote their business.

The expertly handled use of concrete as a finish continues upstairs with the stairwells and lift landing spaces feeling as considered and as special as the office space itself. Doors are held open in recesses to encourage the flow of people, energy and the acoustically baffled noise of busy-ness. Every pair of floors has been considered together in the fire compartment strategy, allowing for double-height spaces between lift lobbies, and corridors vertically breaking the traditional monotony of the typical horizontal commercial plan.

The ambition and level of innovation in the project's brief and concept development is high, and the confidence that the client had in trusting their own instincts and their architect's ideas (as opposed to an agent's advice) should be highly commended. The success of the experimentation is evident in the client's decision to replicate many of the more surprising strategies in their new developments at planning stage.

53 GREAT SUFFOLK STREET

Hawkins\Brown

CLIENT: MORGAN CAPITAL PARTNERS
LOCATION: LONDON, SE1
PHOTOGRAPHY: JIM STEPHENSON

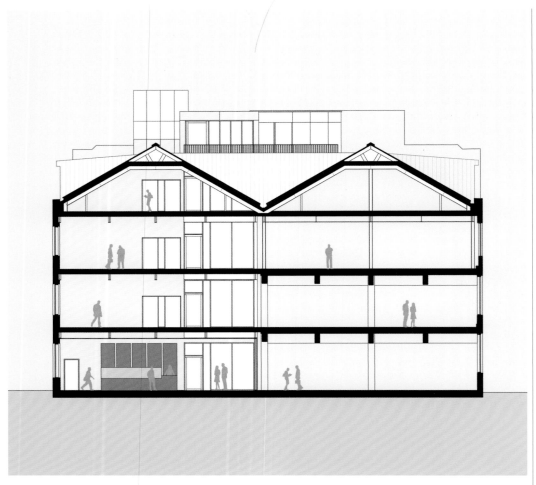

At 53 Great Suffolk Street lies the sensitive refurbishment and extension of a Victorian warehouse, resulting in 40,000 square feet of much needed workspace in Southwark

THE ARCHITECTS HAVE honoured the contextual materials, history and story of the building in the design. The new-build extension takes on the language of the original building, reinterpreting it in a contemporary and confident manner. A palette of quality, crafted materials complements the existing building to create a rich working environment. All are tactile and eye-catching, including the salt-glazed exterior bricks baked in a circular kiln, metal stair and handrail, floor tiles in the bathrooms and on the roof terrace, and the bronze door threshold strips. The shared central staircase is the spine of the building, connecting all floors and office tenants. With its glazed enclosure visible from each office space, this cantilevered raw-steel staircase, complete with brass fittings, is a handsome interior feature.

The architect has worked hard to make the exposed mechanical and electrical services in the office ceilings as beautiful as possible, while the design concept and quality of materials also extend to the basement. The client believed in and supported the architect – clearly they had a great working relationship and are both happy with the finished building.

Every aspect of this office building has been carefully considered, and the palette of materials enhances and complements the raw nature of the existing warehouse building.

KNOX BHAVAN STUDIO

Knox Bhavan Architects

CLIENT: SIMON KNOX & SASHA BHAVAN
LOCATION: LONDON, SE15
PHOTOGRAPHY: DENNIS GILBERT

This building opens up the profession of architecture to a wider audience. Absolutely every aspect of this exquisitely crafted and detailed office design has been thought about

AN ARCHITECTURAL PRACTICE occupies the ground floor of a former stationery shop in a Peckham neighbourhood. On stepping inside you are greeted by a three-storey entry hall accommodating a staircase down to the basement and a steel stair up to a meeting room on a mezzanine level. Every millimetre of space on this small rectangular site has been carefully designed so it works hard and is used effectively.

The excavated basement houses a kitchen, eating area, workshop, sample library, stationery storage and library. Meanwhile, the ground floor houses a small meeting room, WC and studio space for 12 workstations. The well-being of staff was carefully considered, with natural light from two linear roof lights designed in such a way as to avoid any glare on workstation screens. The room has two storage cupboards running down each side, with cupboards for each worker behind their desks. The workstations alone are a exquisitely crafted invention for stand-sit adjustable desks, and are easy to use.

A large south-facing window overlooks the linear koi pond and the courtyard garden beyond. A mirrored brise-soleil cuts out direct sunlight from computer screens and reflects the colourful koi carp in the pond.

From the outside you are greeted by a large concrete-framed bay window which provides a shop-window façade. This façade inspires and delights passers-by – every day people gaze into the shop window (aka office window), stroke the fake grass outside, take a photos of the front façade or knock on the door to come in and see what's inside.

This building provides delight on a daily basis to all those who see it.

THE DEPARTMENT STORE

Squire and Partners

CLIENT: SQUIRE AND PARTNERS
LOCATION: LONDON, SW9
PHOTOGRAPHY: JAMES JONES

This project took an unoccupied and dilapidated former department store, and reimagined the buildings to create a series of inspiring work and social spaces for a multi-disciplinary architecture and design practice

THE BRIEF INCLUDED a series of units for new and existing local businesses, including a community post office, coffee roastery, vinyl record store, delicatessen and bar/restaurant.

It is a stunning building which has been brought back to life: exceedingly exquisite and sensitive restoration, filled with beautiful material choices, attention to details and wonderful spaces.

The project honours the existing building's history by keeping graffiti from squatters, revealing original features and removing paint in order to revert to original colours. All new items added to the building are highlighted in bronze, with an underlying colour scheme of new inserts of gold and black.

The architectural model-making space on the ground floor provides a 'museum of curiosity' type of shop window, providing inspiration to passers-by who can peer inside to see the display of what architects do and how they work.

This development showcases the skills of its architects and interior designers. The building contains an elegant interior design including bespoke desks, storage systems and newly inserted stairs. Equally the interior scheme uses parts of the existing building, such as a large warehouse metal sliding door now used as a magnetic pin-up space. Door threshold strips are from laser-cut plywood made in the workshop, with patterns inspired from the original building.

Workplace well-being was considered throughout, with carefully lit spaces and teams grouped in small clusters. A bar occupies the top floor with a large terrace overlooking Brixton. Round wood columns are used in this timber-structured rooftop pavilion.

Overall, this project's sense of fun has combined with the desire to honour history, and has brought much delight to those who step inside.

25 SAVILE ROW

Piercy&Company

CLIENT: DERWENT LONDON
LOCATION: LONDON, W1
PHOTOGRAPHY: JACK HOBHOUSE

This refurbishment of an Art Deco office is an exquisitely executed project, from the first conceptual move to the finest point of detail

THE OUTLINE BRIEF was to create additional space within a constrained site, in a way that was sympathetic to the building's heritage. For the fit-out, it was to reflect the developer/client's ethos of quality, while also promoting organisational collaboration. The result is a very beautifully crafted, light and elegant building, in which consistent care and thought have gone into every element throughout the briefing, design and construction processes.

The primary spatial move was to cut a three-storey atrium in the middle of the plan, and to suspend within it the lightest of sculptural steel staircases. This has connected volumes of space across floors, with views through and across the whole building, creating a great sense of openness and lightness.

Careful consideration was given to the sustainability strategy for the building. The existing fabric was kept to reduce the overall embodied energy. The building had high levels of thermal mass, and low window-to-wall ratios. Where new spaces were constructed, such as a winter garden and new office penthouse, new walls and roofs have high levels of insulation and consequently high thermal performance. In addition, glazing was analysed using dynamic thermal models to confirm best g-value and thermal performance. The building is generally

mechanically ventilated with heat recovery, using a boiler with 97 per cent efficiency and a high-performing VRV system.

Externally the white render and grid of black steel windows were reconditioned. Into this a beautifully detailed bronze framed entrance was set. The careful detailing is consistent throughout the interior where, as well as bronze, the palette was limited to oak, leather, travertine and steel, with carefully planned juxtapositions between hard-edged semi-industrial elements and more refined, warmer materials. The characteristics of each are explored and exploited, such as a delicate scalloped detail to the oak lining. A defining innovative feature was the exploration of digital craft and collaboration between client, architect and artisan. Intensive design and fabrication workshops were held with expert makers from the outset. This approach of bringing together cutting-edge digital and traditional craftsmanship techniques has created a very beautiful building for the long term, which in an understated way enriches the cityscape in which it sits.

6
SACRED & MONUMENTS

SACRED & MONUMENTS

Sensitivity is important when creating a place of worship or burial: these are sacred spaces that need to transcend their form to point towards a higher realm

For the National Awards we work to the seven key judging criteria laid down by RIBA, and with that in mind I particularly value the three key Vitruvian virtues of 'commodity, firmness and delight'. I'm not sure those criteria for architecture have ever been bettered. I feel particularly strongly about context and creativity in conservation. I am always impressed by those projects where the architects have demonstrated a clear understanding and appreciation of their broad context and immediate setting – whether urban, suburban or rural. For me, such considerations are essential to the success of a project.

Context is a major issue, and when judging a piece of architecture you have to regard the effect on its setting. It's not just the building, it's how it relates to the things around it in terms of height, material and detail. That ties in with RIBA's criteria of making a generous contribution to the public realm. That doesn't necessarily mean it has to be modest. It can be that, or it can be a very strong statement; either way, the architect needs to have shown that he or she has understood the setting in which they are working. I have seen brilliant pieces of architecture if they are viewed in isolation like pieces of sculpture but which are disasters in terms of their impact on their setting. In my view, you must always ensure the external form has a beneficial impact on the setting.

For a long time there has been high quality in the design of new sacred buildings in the UK. It goes right back to the 1960s and 1970s and beyond,

particularly in the Catholic Church and to a lesser extent the Anglican. In recent years there have been a number of new or substantially altered sacred buildings that have come to prominence through the National Awards. This year we have a good crop of sacred buildings that are all very different and all say something important and deserve national recognition.

This is an area of particular interest to me. In my view, conveying the senses of continuity and of the numinous are of fundamental importance in the design of new sacred spaces and buildings or their alteration or extension, and in the design of new memorials. I see these qualities

CONVEYING THE SENSES OF CONTINUITY AND OF THE NUMINOUS ARE OF FUNDAMENTAL IMPORTANCE IN THE DESIGN OF NEW SACRED SPACES AND BUILDINGS

present in the six relevant projects among this year's National and International Awards: the new Durham Cathedral Open Treasure; the new Jewish cemetery at Bushey; the upgrading and enhancement of St Augustine's Church, Hammersmith; the repair and reconstruction of the ancient church of Vilanova de la Barca, Lleida, Catalonia, the Sancaklar Mosque in Turkey, and the Bethnal Green memorial. I discerned them too among some of last year's Awards projects, such as the Vajrasana Buddhist Retreat Centre in Suffolk, the Remembrance Centre at the National Memorial Arboretum in Staffordshire, the Rievaulx Abbey Visitor Centre and Museum

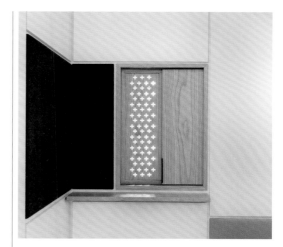

in North Yorkshire, and in the major re-ordering of Wakefield Cathedral.

With sacred buildings, sensitivity is important. Any solution needs to go beyond the purely functional. Whether these places are a church such as St Augustine's, a cemetery as at Bushey or a monument such as at Bethnal Green, they need to meet the needs of their community spiritually. I don't think the architect necessarily needs to be of a particular religious persuasion. A classic example is Edward Cullinan's rebuilding of St Mary's Church in Barnes, completed in 1984 after near complete destruction by fire, the architect being of Jewish background and never having designed a church before. That was a rebuilding, not simply a restoration, and it's one of the most successful sacred buildings I can think of – it's one I'd take to my own desert island.

Importantly too, there is no reason in my view that in adapting historic places of prayer and worship to accommodate additional community or other secular uses need in any way compromise the fundamental liturgical role of the building if carried out with discernment and sensitivity. Up and down the country there are numerous examples of such projects, particularly in Anglican parish churches.

BUSHEY CEMETERY

Waugh Thistleton Architects

CLIENT: THE UNITED SYNAGOGUE
LOCATION: BUSHEY
PHOTOGRAPHY: LEWIS KHAN, SARAH BLEE

Waugh Thistleton have a very strong, long-term relationship with the Jewish community. They have undertaken a number of synagogues prior to this project and the simplicity, austerity even, of the means and materials used in this project is a reflection of this mutual respect, trust and empathy

EVERY ASPECT OF the building layout and progress through the landscape is in keeping with the spirit of the event.

Consistent with the Jewish idea of being buried very simply, in a cardboard coffin, in simple clothes, the buildings carry through the idea of returning the body to the ground, "earth to earth, ashes to ashes". In contrast with the plainness of the buildings, the landscape is almost lush. The cemetery is surrounded by a tree belt and a series of balancing ponds to capture the increased rain-water run-off fed by a cleverly constructed drainage system.

The limited number of buildings, the simplicity of the forms and expressionist choice of materials

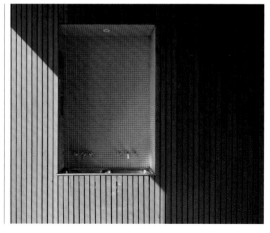

all reflect the symbolism of burial to the Jewish community. An example of the care with which each element has been considered is the gentle slope of the floor in the prayer halls that tips the visitors forward along the route to the graves. This project will be just one stage in the ongoing process of enlarging the cemetery so that the community can continue to honour and protect their dead. The fact that the rammed earth walls of the prayer hall will return to the earth once the cemetery is full and has to be extended again is a poetic response to the programme for the cemetery and the traditions of the Jewish faith.

DURHAM CATHEDRAL OPEN TREASURE

Purcell

CLIENT: DURHAM CATHEDRAL
LOCATION: DURHAM
PHOTOGRAPHY: ANDY MARSHALL

The works to Durham Cathedral are a subtle and elegant addition to the medieval, Grade I listed structure

WORKING WITH THE cathedral staff for over seven years, the architects have created an inspiring visitor experience that celebrates the architecture of the building and showcases its historic collections by remodelling previously hidden spaces.

The sequence of spaces have been carefully adapted to create a range of environmental conditions that respond to the differing needs of the collection, from medieval stonework and book collections through to Anglo-Saxon artefacts.

Bronze stainless-steel and glass lift shafts have been carefully inserted into the existing structure to provide accessible routes throughout, while new timber doors separate and secure the zones. This restricted palette of materials has been used against existing stone structures to provide a timeless, high-quality finish based on traditional craftmanship. This attention to detail reflects the stature and significance of the cathedral.

The design seamlessly integrates historic features and modern interventions that include creative repair and conservation and adaptive reuse of the historic buildings.

The judges were particularly impressed by the quality of the workmanship and detailing, including delicate inclusion of lead-framed secondary glazing to enhance the performance of the structure without affecting its appearance. The joinery throughout, and the subtle integration of new lighting and ventilation systems without visually impacting the historic structure, reinforces an overall sense of accomplishment and skill.

ST AUGUSTINE'S CHURCH

Roz Barr Architects

CLIENT: THE ORDER OF ST AUGUSTINE
LOCATION: FULHAM PALACE ROAD, LONDON, W6
PHOTOGRAPHY: JOHN MACLEAN

This project demonstrates how, with simple moves and extraordinary care and attention, an otherwise unprepossessing building can be transformed – in this case – into a place with a calm, ethereal quality, wholly fitting for a sacred space

IN RESTORING THE building, years of layers of paint and decoration were stripped back from timber and masonry, though with defects left exposed. Wood in the vestibule and a very dark stained roof in the chapel were also stripped back, sanded and treated with a white oil, with the original black steel fixings waxed and left in place. This has created an almost Shaker-like aesthetic of lightness, simplicity and purity. New confession booths were formed, delicately detailed to echo the form of the internal vaulted ceilings. The floor level of the altar was raised and reconfigured, with a large slab of green marble, which must have sat rather heavily as a backdrop to one of the side altars, transformed by being carefully integrated into the high altar floor. Combined with a large, beautifully formed cast-iron circular light fitting, this subtly defines the aura of the high altar, reinforced by a very delicate fresco, hand-painted and depicted in gold leaf on the rear wall of the altar. The architect's fruitful collaboration with artisans and makers permeates this project, with the focus being the high altar itself, a strong simple form in blood-red Venetian plaster, by the ceramicist Julian Stair.

An innovative heating system has been introduced, with heating pipes embedded in the masonry walls, with the intention of creating a more sustainable and efficient solution to servicing historic fabric than is usual. The principle is that, since the church has a very large volume and occasional use,

copper heating pipes embedded just below the window sills will heat the walls, which will radiate heat at congregation level. The effect should be to raise the radiant temperature while lowering the air temperature as one moves up the wall. The results are still being monitored for temperature, comfort and energy expenditure, as part of a long-term assessment. By warming the heavyweight walls, the internal moisture was reduced, which in turn reduced the overall U-value of the walls. This helped eliminate rising damp within the historic structure.

On this project, the effect of very careful stripping away and subtle restoration, combined with beautiful and accomplished detailing and the addition of exquisitely crafted sacred elements, has transformed a mediocre building into a place with a transcendental quality, expressed through the human effort of making simple things very special.

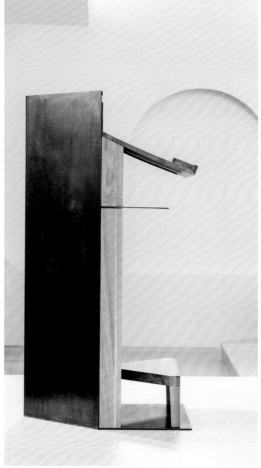

COLEM... GEAR... HIL...
HIGGINSON JULIER LEWIS NEWTON LOFTUS
LEGGETT PRICE
NEWMAN POOLE
REYNOLDS
SHARP
PELF
SEAR
SPEIGHT
THOMPSON
TROTTER

BETHNAL GREEN MEMORIAL

Arboreal Architecture

CLIENT: STAIRWAY TO HEAVEN MEMORIAL TRUST
LOCATION: LONDON, E2
PHOTOGRAPHY: MARCELA SPADARO

In 1943, one of the worst civilian disasters in modern British history occurred in what is now the south-east access stair to Bethnal Green Underground station, used at the time as an air raid shelter during World War II

DURING ONE AIR RAID, a total of 173 people (including 62 children and babies) were crushed and asphyxiated to death as they rushed to gain shelter.

With an even greater death toll than the 1966 Aberfan landslide, and the 1989 Hillsborough stadium disaster, it is surprising that so few nowadays know about this tragedy. An official inquiry was held days after it happened but was kept secret until after the war. Despite censored press reports at the time, those involved were told by officials not to talk about it, and the story was suppressed for fear of undermining the war effort. In the absence of the truth, rumours spread that a German bomb had landed in the stairwell, which was convenient accidental propaganda was allowed to prosper.

In 1945 the inquiry report was released, but even so, the witness statements and various documents – including those outlining requests to the Home Secretary to improve the safety and condition of the stairwell before the disaster – continued to be classified and have only recently been made public.

Many of those directly affected by the incident, partly due to the authorities reaction, and partly because of the terror and trauma of the experience, suppressed the event, never talking about it, even to their families.

In 2006, 63 years after the event, Bethnal Green architect Harry Paticas noticed a plaque that had been discreetly fixed to the stair in 1993, quietly acknowledging the deaths. After some research, he felt strongly that a more fitting memorial was needed to better acknowledge the tragedy for those who were killed, as well as their families and those who survived.

What followed was an 11-year labour of compassion. It began with a good deal of research, investigation, revelations, meeting victims' families and survivors (some telling their story to their

families for the first time), and the emergence of a charity client in 2008 – Stairway to Heaven Memorial Trust – to raise money for the project. Subsequently there was charity tin rattling, political lobbying and negotiations with TfL (regarding their stairwell and tunnels below) Thames Water (about the water main below), and statutory authorities (on the subject of the gas and electric main below).

The design concept was an inversion of the negative space within the stairwell where the crush occurred, lifted up and to one side of the stairwell in the corner of Bethnal Green's nearby park. The hollowed-out negative stairwell is built from sustainably sourced solid teak with conical shaped holes in the roof that, at midday, throw light shafts toward the stairwell where the tragedy occurred, one for each life lost. A polished concrete plinth supports the teak inverted stair, and folds across the site with multiple bronze plates fixed to it with extracts from the accounts of survivors and victims' families. The plinth twists and leads to a bench where those who have just read the accounts can pause and reflect.

The outcome of the project, 11 years after Harry Paticas noticed the small plaque, is a striking memorial that is part sculpture and part architecture, with considerable intellectual conceptual rigour. It is a poignant justification for its form, permitting and considering the viewer's experience and spatial interaction. Structurally complex, it has been constructed and completed to an impeccable level of finish and detail.

The project would not have happened without the architect going way beyond the extent of simply 'doing his job'. He created the project from nothing, he researched and established his brief, he discovered the people who he would need to be the client, he helped the client to fundraise and shake tins, and he engaged in complex negotiations with multiple parties which one would normally have to do for a significant building project (and a significant fee). In short, he found a way to achieve the memorial and succeeded.

INDEX

ARCHITECTS AND BUILDINGS

CREDITS

RIBA
Mike Clarke
Matthew Dobson
Imogen Grubin
Mica Jones
Juliet Leach
Carmen Mateu-Moreno
Marcelo Ventura

Photography
Keith Barnes
Tony Barwell
Sarah Blee
broad daylight
Richard Byrant
Mark Carline
Anthony Coleman
Peter Cook
Tim Crocker
Johan Dehlin
Ståle Eriksen
Richard Fraser
Graham Gaunt
Dennis Gilbert
Ross Gillespie
Ian Goodfellow
David Grandorge
Aaron Hargreaves
Jack Hobhouse
Hufton + Crow
Keith Hunter
James Jones

Tom Kahler
Lewis Khan
Nick Kane
Quintin Lake
Peter Landers
John MacLean
Tricia Malley
John Maltby
Andy Marshall
James Newman
Jason Orton
Dimitris Panagioditis
Rob Parrish
Alex Peacock
Paul Raftery
Paul Riddle
Alex de Rijke
Heini Schneebeli
Adam Scott
Peter Shannon
Toby Smith
Tim Soar
Jasmin Sohi
Joas Souza
Marcela Spadaro
Jim Stephenson
Stillview Photography
Greg Storrar
John Sturrock
Paul White
Alan Williams
Nigel Young

All other images are provided
courtesy of the architects.

Design
Artifice Press

Writing
John Lewis
Justin Lewis
Peter Watts

Proofreading
Liz Jones

© 2018 Artifice Press Limited, the architects,
photographers and the authors.
All rights reserved.

Artifice Press Limited
298 Regents Park Road, London, N3 2SZ
United Kingdom

+44 (0)20 8371 4000
office@artificeonline.com
www.artificeonline.com

All opinions expressed within this publication are those
of the authors and not necessarily of the publisher.

British Library in Cataloguing Data
A CIP record for this book is available from the British Library.

ISBN 978-1-911339-30-4

No part of this publication may be reproduced, stored in a
retrieval system, or transmitted, in any form or by any means,
electronic, mechanical, photocopying, recording, or otherwise,
without prior permission of the publisher.

Every effort has been made to trace the copyright holders,
but if any have been inadvertently overlooked the necessary
arrangements will be made at the first opportunity.

Artifice Press is an environmentally responsible company.
This book is printed on sustainably sourced paper.

Printed by CPi Colour, London.